Once Upon a Yogi Time

Tales of the Siddhis

by

Phillip Hurley

Maithuna Publications

2016

Once Upon a Yogi Time:
Tales of the Siddhis

Maithuna Publications is an imprint of:
> Good Idea Creative Services
> 324 Minister Hill Road
> Wheelock VT 05851 USA

ISBN: 978-0-9984727-0-6

Library of Congress Control Number: 2016920352

Library of Congress subject heading:
> Yogis--United States--Biography

Author's website:

www.tantrayoga.us

अ

Contents

Preface

"Geniis are intelligent complexes of energy, same as you or I, and just as real.

"You can contact them and they will respond to you."

It was a beautiful June day in Vermont, and we sat on the grass under a large maple tree on a hillside on the western edge of the Green Mountains. I had driven several hours to get there, through narrow winding valleys and over steep mountain passes, from my home in the northeastern part of the state.

And now, here I was, sitting with a person quite different from anyone I had ever known, and yet more familiar to me than my own family.

Who was this tall handsome man with brown curly hair, high cheekbones, chiseled features and Slavic eyes?

I first met him when he read my astrological natal chart, at the suggestion of a mutual friend. The reading was delivered without pretension in a very low-key, matter of fact way – and totally spot-on. In my head I was just going along with a slightly blase attitude of, "Oh yes of course…" until at some point, toward the end of the reading, it occurred to me, "Wait a minute – this person has never met me before, and yet he is describing my inmost thought and emotional patterns in accurate detail." It caught me off guard, to say the least, and I was quite fascinated.

I'd had an intense interest in yoga and things paranormal since my childhood, but I had lived most of my life in a rural, isolated area, where information and people resources were quite limited in this realm. It was long before the days of the internet.

I had strong intuitive faculties, and though I flirted with various groups – Silva Mind Control, Arica, Wiccans, Taoists, Pagans, Buddhists – there was always something that felt not-quite-right about them, so I kept pretty much to myself in terms of spiritual practice.

But this was something else, with a genuineness and depth of practical intelligence I had not felt elsewhere. I absolutely wanted to learn more.

And so, here I was with Phillip Hurley

"You can do a 'formal' ritual, if you like, for evocation or invocation; or, if you understand that every movement in time and space is ritual, you can simply call on a genii as you would another person, in a conversational manner, if you will.

"The 360 geniis of the zone girdling the earth are quite easy to work with. They correspond to the 360 degrees of the zodiac, and each has its particular characteristics and capabilities.

"Let's try Sumuram, 27 degrees Virgo, who has to do with birds and other flying creatures. Sumuram, let's see some hawks!" Index finger erect, his right hand whirled a vortex, spiraling upward from his chest to above his head, a signature gesture of his.

"Interesting," I thought to myself, casting my eyes all around above the tree line, "but, hawks are not at all unusual to see in this area at this time of the year... But, anyway, let's see..."

The conversation moved on, as I had many questions, and the evocation of Sumuram was forgotten.

Later, we set out through the woods to a swimming hole in the river, scrambling down steep boulder-strewn slopes amid old-growth hardwoods.

I have always felt most at home in the woods. As a child, forests, fields and mountains were my playground. Here, I was becoming engrossed in spotting botany and fungi new to me, when we heard a high pitched whistle, very near by.

Just skimming the treetops above us was a broad-winged hawk... but wait, no, there were two hawks, a pair, and they were following us, gliding from tree to tree. I had never seen this kind of behavior before. What the...?

They continued to follow us closely for a considerable distance. They did not seem at all distressed, as you would expect if we had come too close to their nest and they were trying to run us off. They were just... following us. I kept looking over my shoulder up at them, slowing our progress to our destination. I wanted to just stop and hang out to see what they would do. This was all quite fascinating to me.

Phil barely batted an eye at them. Soon, he became ever so slightly impatient.

"You're more interested in those hawks than you are in me!"

"No, no, it's just that, well, I've never seen anything like this before. I mean, I've seen a lot of hawks, but not following me around like this. It's really cool! So that's Sumuram, huh?!"

"Sure, and there are legions more. All you have to do is put your consciousness into akasha and you can access them..." He smiled wryly.

– Leigh Hurley 2016

Introduction

Many years ago, as a very young man, I took the first conscious steps of my spiritual journey. It began by reading a few books, doing a little meditation, and being initiated by a siddha guru swami. Each subsequent step has led me deeper into magical realms.

Siddhi is a Sanskrit word that refers to the attainment of magical power beyond normal human experience, and is generally used in the context of the practice of yoga. Typically today, citing the writings of Patanjali, the aspiring yogi is sternly warned against using or seeking out such powers. However, there is much more to yoga than Patanjali. Although gaining siddhis is not the essential goal of yoga, it doesn't hurt to have a little fun on the way to cosmic consciousness, and indeed, in India, traditionally, yogis are associated with siddhis, and the use of them.

The stories I relate to you in this book are not fantasy. I am mentally sound. I don't take drugs and none of the experiences or states of consciousness presented here was the result of taking of any drug, or shamanic brew. Fact is indeed stranger than fiction.

I am an average person with an interest in yoga. I pursued that interest with study and practice, though I did not really go out of my way, nor was I an ascetic. In all honesty, my efforts were sporadic, but I have an inner compass that has kept me on course (though sometimes in a round-about way) as a yogi. My interest has always been keen, and my persistence over time has rewarded me with an abundance of experiences that could be called "supernatural."

Most of the vignettes in this book occurred when I was just getting started on my esoteric journey. They are not presented in chronological order.

For the yogi, there are other dimensions of time and space to be experienced, beyond our physical plane, waking state of consciousness. For the purposes of my stories, I will describe and divide these dimensions of time and space simply into four main divisions: etheric, astral, mental, and causal - essentially the Western occult model.

In case you are not familiar with yogic and occult lore, at the back of this book you will find a more detailed discussion of this four-fold breakdown, as well as a brief discussion of other models for the different dimensions of time and space. I hope it will help make the experiences I will be relating to you easier to understand.

The Alchemist

For me, the journal was truly eye candy. It evoked the distant past with medieval woodcuts of alchemists toiling over alembics and furnaces, surrounded by mysterious sigils; and it brought that past into present-day reality with photos of modern alchemists in white lab coats, surrounded by soxhlet extractors, cold presses, and all the accoutrements of a well-equipped laboratory – all on smooth, glossy paper. At the time I believe it was called *The Alchemical Laboratory Bulletin,* and I was quite taken in by its allure.

I had been studying tantric alchemy with my guru Goswami Kriyananda at the College of Occult Sciences in Chicago. I had also recently completed studies with Emerson College of Herbology (one of the first schools of herbal medicine in North America) and what I must call formidable training in astrology by Ernest and Catherine Grant, founders of the American Federation of Astrologers.

I was engaged in further studies at the COS in hermetics, quabbalah, Sanskrit and other disciplines as well. Although I was still very young, and wet behind the ears, I was enthusiastic, and a fast learner. My training and spiritual discipline as an initiate of Goswami Kriyananda was exponentially expanding my knowledge and I was developing some amazing skills.

All of this was a solid foundation for further studies and practice in the art of alchemy. I was in the process of writing a book, *Herbal Alchemy,* and I knew that I needed some more comprehensive and practical physical lab experience than was available to me at the time in Chicago. I wanted to clarify and enhance my own techniques, and I also looked forward to learning something new.

The Alchemical Labratory Bulletin was published by Paracelsus Research Society and Albert Riedel, who was also known as Frater Albertus, the founder of the organization.

I was already involved in deep study and practice of Ayurveda for producing gem bhasmas and working with plant materials, but I lacked the equipment to further my practical work and study at the physical level. I also thought it would be exciting to meet and work with other people who had the same interests.

I exchanged a few letters with Albertus inquiring about studying with him, and spoke with him on the phone several times. Ultimately, I decided to make the 1400 mile trip to Salt Lake City, Utah where he lived and had his laboratory. I signed up for a two-week course at Paracelsus Research.

In preparation I read Albertus' book, *The Alchemist's Handbook*. It did not actually have anything in it that I had not already learned at the COS, but I could tell that his physical laboratory techniques were sophisticated and excellent for preparing plant material. I was, however, slightly bothered that the book included no foundation or root philosophy. This seemed strange to me, as one does not make progress in the work of alchemy without attending to that first. Still, I was undeterred by this qualm, and was excited to begin my new adventure in the glitzy world of expensive lab equipment and who knows what else.

I found a ride through a ride-board and set out for Utah.

The drive overland through Iowa, Nebraska and Wyoming was not eventful. The scenery was a change from the streets of Chicago, but for the most part, it was not the best each of these states has to offer. The only remarkable thing that occurred during the trip was being stopped on the highway by a police officer in Nebraska because I looked suspicious. I had a full head of curly long hair, and at that time in the more rural and conservative parts of the country, people were not accustomed to seeing my type. The police officer was actually very polite, but it was clear I was an "outsider."

As we approached Salt Lake City, I was refreshed by the beauty of the Wasatch Mountains in the distance. They were a visual relief after all the long, wide flat expanses we had just traversed.

I was dropped off in the city's outskirts at the Paracelsus Research Society, a collection of a few architecturally unremarkable 1950s-style buildings. As I walked into the central courtyard, I detected no signs of human life in any of the buildings. The place was apparently deserted.

On one side of the courtyard I noticed in passing a small newly-paved parking area that appeared to have never been driven on. But my full attention was captured by a statue covered with a bed sheet. It stood at the edge of a small pool in another part of the courtyard, and was quite eerie-looking. It gave me a spooky feeling, and I wondered why it was draped.

I walked up to the statue. The pool was empty of water, filled with dry leaves only. I lifted the sheet. The statue was decapitated, with the head now visible on the ground at its feet.

This strange omen gave me a chill, and I knew it was a prognostication of this venture. I needed to be on my guard.

Still, I shook off the foreboding, and chose to dwell in my enthusiasm for soxhelet extractors and the anticipated company of other alchemists. I had plenty of time for this, as it was two or three hours before I saw the first stirrings of life.

A thin, mercurial figure moved quickly toward me, brandishing a cleaning rag. She had an unsettled look about her, like things were never quite right and she had to be ready to fix them when the disorder revealed itself. Her approach was swift and her manner, to the point. "Are you here for the classes?"

I detected a German accent. "Yes," I replied.

"OK, I show you where you stay."

I was led to a single-floor motel-like structure with two rooms separated by a common room in between them.

"This will be your room." She opened a door and ushered me in.

We shared some small talk, while she continuously dusted everything in her sight. At that point I realized that her rag was her calling card, and indeed, I never saw her without a cleaning rag in hand.

The lady with the rag, who I later learned was Frater Albertus' wife Emmy, had told me that classes would begin at 8:00 a.m. sharp the next morning, so I had time to decompress, read a little and just relax. The room was nice, several chairs, a good size bed, and of course, all of it dusted with a rag to perfect cosmic cleanliness.

Getting a sense of my new surroundings was not easy. The place seemed pleasant enough, but after all, it was Salt Lake City. The vibe was significantly more conservative than I was used to, and felt quite foreign to me. I had no idea what to expect, but anyway, I unpacked my bag and lay on the bed to meditate.

As I fell asleep for the night, images of the headless statue filled the spaces between my thoughts.

I hate getting up early in the morning. I'm a night person, so much that I have been asked quite seriously if I was a vampire. Of course I replied in the negative, but I have to admit it was a reserved "no," as one can never be quite sure exactly what the members of one's ancestral bloodlines were up to.

So, I was not pleased that I was going to have to get up at 7:00 a.m. on what I considered to be a sort of vacation. When the time came, I talked myself out of bed, climbed into some rather rumpled clothes and aimed myself across the courtyard towards the building that housed the classrooms and laboratory.

Faces emerged from the shadows of the shrubbery in front of the building.

There were a few short hellos, and stealthy, silent sizing-up of each other. The eight of us shared awkward smiles and stared off into the distance, eagerly anticipating the arrival of the mysterious Frater Albertus.

Finally, a man of about 60, bespectacled and wearing a cardigan sweater, walked briskly through the courtyard towards us.

Beneath a protruding brow were two inquisitive eyes that engaged you directly, even if only for an instant. He had a prominent nose that fit in well with the rest of his rugged features.

He acknowledged us curtly, pointed the key in the direction of the lock, and, with a twist and a turn, the door to the lab was open.

We were led swiftly past rows of soxhlet extractors, sand baths and other intriguing devices, into a classroom with chairs arranged around a table for the initial class.

Albertus sat on a desk in front of us and began fiddling with a letter opener which was shaped like a miniature sword.

He opened with a warm welcome to the season's sessions, then took a lengthy pause, gazing intently upon each of us in turn. Then, to our total amazement, he suddenly thrust his letter-opener sword up into the air, and uttered loudly and fervently, "The Archangels can CRRUSH you."

But, before we could even begin to process that statement, it was punctuated by a loud, "Baa-aa-aaa, baa-aa-aaa" issuing through the walls, as one of the neighbor's sheep commented on the proceedings. The timing was superb – unintentional high comedy at its best. After the initial shock, we had to muster all of our strength to keep from breaking out in uproarious laughter. We all sneaked glances at our fellow classmates to note the reactions to this bizarre presentation.

Taking no notice of being upstaged by a sheep, Albertus continued with his very emotionally charged theme of archangels, and basically what low worms we mortals are, and how easily we all could be disposed of by higher forces.

He did eventually change the subject and returned to a more normal class orientation, discussing the class plan for the coming weeks, and the expectations and rules.

All in all, the class group was well balanced in that it had four women and four men, with a good representation of different generations, lifestyles, and cultures. Most were polite and seemed ready to engage in conversation, with a few who were reserved and quiet, but certainly friendly.

Back in my room after the orientation, I lay on the bed thinking about the curious events of the day and the interesting people I had met. As I drifted into a deep sleep I couldn't let go of my impression of Albertus' wackiness, but I reasoned with myself that that was OK since my interest in the class was just to learn plant preparation techniques.

I woke up early, which was quite unusual for me, but, after all, I was in a strange place, surrounded by people I did not know. This imparted extra energy to my aura and made me more alert and awake.

I was still lying in bed when suddenly the door opened and Emmy and her rag appeared. I kept still and watched through half-closed eyes as she entered the room without saying a word or acknowledging my presence, and dusted the dresser and straightened out the doily on it. She moved on to several other items, giving them the business with her rag. Then, as suddenly as she appeared, she disappeared, leaving the room without a word.

"Well, that was a bit odd, wasn't it?" I thought to myself.

I rousted myself, got up and out, and was on my way to another day.

In class we were given many large, full color handouts to study, and assignments to go along with them. We were also introduced to the lab equipment and lab procedures.

Days passed and I was happily engaged in the processes of gathering, preparing and separating, and recombining plant constituents. This was what I came for and this is what I was getting. There was so much to do with study assignments that I did not have an opportunity to socialize until a number of days had passed since our orientation.

I was sitting outdoors and enjoying the nice weather when I saw Emmy vigorously sweeping the new parking area in the courtyard. I decided to go over and chat. As I approached, I could hear her mumbling to herself, but I could not quite make out what she was saying. She was clearly disturbed about something.

As I got closer, she looked up at me and said, "I don't see why they have to use this driveway. It just gets it dirty!"

With no recognition of my presence except for this remark, she continued to sweep away at the barely noticeable light grey dirt marks left by tires upon the driveway.

I realized that I was not going to get the sort of conversation I was looking for, and decided to return to my seat in the courtyard. As an astrologer, the only thing I could think of as I watched her sweep was that she was a Virgo run amok. I mean if you can't drive in a driveway…. ?

I should not have been surprised. I was becoming increasingly suspicious of the behavior exhibited by Frater Albertus. He was up one minute and down the next in big ways. He seemed to have a rather inflated sense of himself and his mission. I decided to give him a wide berth. I kept to my business, did my work and did not ask him questions. I noticed that when esoteric questions were put to him by students, he only answered in riddles, and his replies had more than a tinge of sarcasm. Most of these non-answers, given with a wry look, were, I think, intended to convey that he possessed a hidden wisdom, which, I was beginning to discover, was not actually there.

One evening a few days into the course, I decided to socialize and went to the common room in the dormitory building, where most of my classmates were staying.

We sat around sharing our stories, and since we were all students of alchemy, the conversation inevitably turned to the topic of transmutation, and materialization and de-materialization. I had been studying and working with these processes, and making significant progress back in Chicago, and I thought of them as quite ordinary for someone study-ing alchemy to be involved in. They are, after all, the core alchemical processes, are they not? So, I was not reticent to talk about my experiences.

Several people asked me to materialize something for them as they had never witnessed such phenomena before.

I agreed to materialize a scent for anyone who asked. Each specified a scent, and I produced it. I was greatly amused by the incredulous looks on their faces.

One of the more ubiquitous minor siddhis that can arise from the practice of yoga is the ability to materialize scents.

My guru Kriyananda used to tell a story. Every time he went to India he crossed paths with a particular yogi looking for alms. The yogi would approach my guru and ask what kind of scent he would like, and then the yogi would ma-terialize it for him. After several encounters over the years, the yogi once again approached Kriyananda and went into exactly the same routine, asking him what scent he wanted.

At that point Kriyananda was a little annoyed, and looked at him and said, "After all these years are you still doing the same old thing?"

Anyway, I honestly enjoyed myself that night, and it seemed that so did the rest of my companions.

There was a couple from California who were a bit more avant garde than the rest of the group, and more like my circle of friends in Chicago.

Charles and Barbara had missed the materialization performance, but heard rave reviews, and they approached me the next evening and asked if I would materialize a scent for them. They sat down in front of me, and I sat so that we faced each other. I asked them what scent they would like and then – nothing happened. It was quite embarrassing – it just did not work. I tried several times – but nothing!

This was the first time my capabilities failed me, but it was not to be the last. I apologized profusely, and they said they understood. Barbara was very psychic as well as very good-looking. She told me that she saw a square form over one of my eyes and a circle over the other as I attempted to materialize the scent. I found this very interesting as I had never gotten this type of feedback before.

I did notice, however, Barbara's thighs, as I was trying to materialize a scent. She wore a very short skirt and, well, I just could not avoid eye grazing. I now wonder if my little show was highjacked by that pair of sumptuous thighs. Maybe, but I have no regrets…

We all talked for quite a while that evening, enjoying each others' company.

On the way back to my room I mused on a story my guru told me about a well known swami who apparently had a great fear of women because of his sexual attraction to them. His fear of losing his swami powers in the presence of attractive women was so great that every time he flew on an airplane he would either pay for every seat on the plane or at least as many seats around him as possible to avoid having to be seated near a woman. My guru would then say that this was not the yogi way to do things.

The swami should have embraced his fear by throwing himself into the action and mastering his own behavior and reactions. Only then could he truly be called a swami.

I laughed to myself and thought "Well, I am going to have to throw myself into a lot more thighs while I am trying to materialize things so I get this right."

I went to sleep that night with a smile on my face.

The next day we all had a chance to leave the compound and venture into Salt Lake City for a little break from classes. While there, I walked into a candle, bath and general knick-knack shop. As I wandered through the shop, a head popped up from behind the shelf separating the aisles. It was George, one of the students for whom I had materialized a sandlewood scent. He immediately recognized me. His face turned a little red and he had a rather sheepish look.

I greeted him and asked him if he was shopping for something special. He stammered a bit and then said, "Well not exactly, I just wanted to smell some sandlewood soap to see if it was the same scent that you materialized for me last night."

I laughed and said, "Well, is it?"

He said "Yup, that's it all right."

The day that followed proved to be even more intriguing. That evening I was summoned to Albertus' house. I crossed the courtyard, knocked on the door, was let in and led to the kitchen by Emmy. She bade me sit on a kitchen chair by the table, where there were already several people from the class seated. She disappeared, then returned. Frater Albertus entered, and greeted us cursorily.

He did not waste any time, and did not even sit down, but stood leaning back against a kitchen counter alongside Emmy.

He said to me, point blank, "I have heard you materialized some scents last night. Could you materialize something for me?"

I became a little concerned as things did not feel quite right. My intuition told me to say "no," and that I did. But, I also told him that if he would like, I'd gladly teach him how to materialize scents himself, which to my mind was a far better offer.

For some reason my response seemed to throw him. He was silent for quite a while and did not acknowledge the offer. My very strong impression of his silence was that he would not make the request as it would compromise his sense of authority, which he wanted to maintain at all costs.

Instead, he changed the subject and the conversation progressed on to some of the courses I was teaching in Chicago. I mentioned that one of them was astral projection.

A gasp burst out from Emmy when I said the words, and she hissed, "Black magic!!!!"

I was dumbfounded.

Albertus turned sharply toward Emmy and with a loud "Shhhhhhh" put her to silence.

Something told me to keep talking as if nothing odd had happened, and so I did. I also knew that I had to get myself out of that kitchen as soon as possible, but in a polite way, so as to not arouse animosity or create problems. I quickly wound up the conversation by stating that I was tired and needed to study for class the next day.

On the surface the incident seemed to end well, but Emmy's outburst was the revealing keynote of the evening and an omen of what was to come.

The next day's classes were uneventful although I could feel tension in the air. After classes ended in the late afternoon, I went to my room for a short nap before having dinner. I had just barely dozed off when I was awakened by a soft knock on my door.

I got up and opened the door to discover Evelyn, my classmate, who had the room on the other side of the common room of our building. She was disturbed and had an anxious look upon her face.

I said hello, but before I could say anything else she said, "Have you seen my insulin?"

Bewildered, I said, "What?"

"My insulin! It disappeared. I can't find my insulin."

Not knowing what to say because I had no idea why she would be asking me this question, I hesitated in order to gather my wits. I finally comprehended that she had misplaced or lost her insulin.

"I had put it in my dresser drawer, but now it's gone!"

I understood the seriousness of the matter for her well-being, and asked if she had searched the floor in her room, as she might have dropped it. She said she had.

I said, "Well, let's go look again together, and see if we can find it."

As we walked across the common room she blurted out, "They said you dematerialized it!"

I was stunned by the statement and stopped dead in my tracks. My mind went blank as I searched intuitively for the meaning of what she had just said. A quick flash of insight told me, one, that she was referring to my ability to materialize things and thus an assumption was made that I could dematerialize things; and, two, someone considers me a very not-nice person. Emmy hissing, "Black magic!" the night before immediately came to mind. I then realized who "they" were.

I wanted to ask Evelyn about her statement, but the urgency of locating the missing bottle of medication took precedence. I was alarmed for her health and well-being; and, now, secondarily, I was alarmed for myself if we could not locate the missing bottle.

We entered the room. I quickly looked around and Evelyn showed me the drawer where she kept the insulin. Feeling a sense of urgency, I moved the dresser, got down on all fours and visually scoured the area. The bed was very close to the dresser with just enough space to stand between them. I lifted up the blanket which draped over the bed to the floor, and looked under the bed. Hidden behind the bed skirt and barely visible on the floor was the bottle of insulin. It was very small, and because it was clear with just a tiny label on it, it could easily disappear into any background pattern.

With great relief I grabbed the bottle, got up and said, "I found it."

Her anxiety melted and her sense of calm was restored immediately.

Then, she kept repeating that she could not understand how the bottle wound up on the floor under the bed. But I could see that she could have easily pulled a piece of clothing out of the drawer and flipped the bottle onto the floor without noticing; and, Evelyn had that sort of Piscean personality.

She could not seem to get to the point where she realized that she was the direct cause of her own misfortune, so I decided it was time to depart and leave her to it. I politely retired with a smile, but feeling uneasy.

Back in my room I laid down on the bed to rest and think about the incident. I blanked out my mind, and then it came to me in a flash: it was not good that I was the one who found the insulin, because it was whispered that I had dematerialized it! At that moment I realized that the uneasy feeling I had back in Evelyn's room was due to the fact that she actually thought I had rematerialized the bottle and faked finding it under the bed.

This was getting very complicated very fast. I began to think about and understand the mechanisms behind the Salem witch trials and the witch hunts of the Catholic Inquisition. People have a tendency to react to unusual phenomenon with superstition and fear, and there are always those who are eager to fan the flames and point to scape goats.

It was quite frightening. Because I materialized something and talked about astral projection I was immediately branded a "black magician." Thus, I became responsible for any calamity that transpired in people's lives after that revelation. Not only that, but the very people who claimed to be alchemists, and who were teaching alchemy, were the ones promoting this absurd notion. Now, anyone who is a yogi and occultist – in other words, a real alchemist – knows beyond a doubt that materialization is a simple process of transmuting energy to matter. It is not an "evil" thing and not "black magic" as Soror Emmy blurted out.

At this point I realized that these people knew absolutely nothing about what they claimed to know. I was in the midst of people who certainly did not have my best interests at heart, and I urgently needed to be on guard. There are few things worse than a bunch of half-witted pseudo-occultists flailing around like chickens with their heads cut off.

Kriyananda once told a friend of mine, "your ignorance of what you're doing is greater than your knowledge of what you're doing," and while that, of course, goes for all of us at one time or another, I was here experiencing a veritable Niagara Falls of ignorance.

I nervously wondered if they were about to put me in a sack and toss me into a river to see whether I floated or drowned. Float - you're a witch. Drown – you're not a witch, oops, so sorry!

I had trouble sleeping that night, disturbed that people could be so primitive and superstitious; and I was up early the next morning meditating to balance myself a bit amidst the emotional chaos.

As I dressed for the day's classes I became more and more annoyed at what appeared to me to be a preposterous sham. I was losing all enthusiasm for the classes, and was simply not in a good mood about this whole affair.

I walked into class with a bad attitude. Fortunately no one talked to me. My edginess wore off gradually, and I was finally able to concentrate on the class work.

Later that day, after classes, I was in the commons area of the dormitory building where there were cooking facilities. I was sitting on a chair at a table when Shreya came into to prepare some food. She was a Rosicrucian and had come all the way from India to take the class. She was staying with Albertus as a guest in his house. I greeted her with a smile and a hello, but that was returned with a very weak smile and a muffled response which I could not make out.

She did all she could to avoid making eye contact with me and it was apparent that she wanted to avoid talking with me.

I felt like a pariah. I attempted further conversation with her, but her tone was sharp and turning toward nasty. I stared at her in disbelief for a few seconds, then after a few minutes of silence, I excused myself and left the building.

As I walked down the path toward my room I was aggravated and weary of the witch-hunting mentality. But, I tried to give Shreya the benefit of the doubt. Perhaps her coldness was because she felt a social obligation to align herself with Albertus and Emmy since she was a guest in their house. I imagined that it might be hard for her to be so far away from home, and that, under different circumstances, she might be friendlier.

I crawled into bed and was lying on my back, just staring into nothingness, wondering what to do next in this very strange situation. Suddenly a face appeared a few feet past the foot of the bed. It gave me quite a start, so much so that I could not move a muscle except that my eyes opened wide in disbelief. The phantom head was very clear, and it was Shreya. As I realized who it was, I felt a very sharp needle prick on my butt. My body elevated into the air above the mattress by several inches, if not a half a foot. My body was stiff and straight the whole time, with my arms at my sides – not a muscle moved. I simply was levitated into the air. My body fell back onto the mattress and the face dissolved as quickly as it had appeared. I continued to lie there, moving my eyes around the room waiting for something else to happen, but apparently that was all there was to it.

After collecting my wits, I realized that I had just been psychically attacked by Shreya, and she wanted me to know that she was the one who did the deed. Why she would do such a thing, I don't know, but she did... and now the ball was in my court.

My guru, bless his magical soul, knowing that there are people with such capabilities and that some will use them against you for no good reason, gave me a technique for just this sort of situation. I applied it quickly. I was quite astounded as my room filled with energy and lights. I had not used this particular technique before and was really enjoying the pyrotechnics that went with it. The phenomenon continued for about fifteen minutes before the room grew dark again. I stayed awake for several hours looking around the room expecting something else to happen, but apparently it was over and I fell asleep.

The next morning in class, I noticed Shreya was missing. I wondered where she was. Just as I completed that thought, I overheard one of the students say that Shreya had become very ill last night and was in bed, and a doctor had been summoned.

She was bedridden for three days, and then mysteriously departed for India without seeing any classmates or finishing her course of study. I silently thanked my guru for his very effective technique and continued on with my business without further psychic interference.

In India, in some families, mantric formulas are handed down generation to generation. Such mantras can produce their effects without the user ever having to do any discipline or spiritual training. This can be the equivalent of giving an idiot child a loaded gun. Siddhis gained in this fashion can be quite detrimental to the users and more of a curse than a benefit if the user has no ethical training.

This reminded me of the experience that brought Sir John Woodroffe to a serious study of tantra kundalini in his early years as a judge in India in the late 19th century. He had been presiding over a particular court case, and found his deliberations to be uncharacteristically unsettled. He realized that he was being influenced in strange ways, being pulled drastically in favor of one litigant, and then just as quickly began to favor the other litigant. This see-saw effect was dizzying and did not make any sense.

It was a very intense experience for him, and caused him to investigate the situation more deeply. He ultimately discovered that both sides in the litigation were deploying mantras, probably family heirlooms, to influence him.

The powerful effect these mantras had upon him launched his study of tantra, which was to last a lifetime, during which time he authored and translated some of the first English texts about tantra.

For the next three days I plodded along with the program, and by that time I had gotten all the information I needed for the use of laboratory equipment and techniques. I was impressed with Albertus' knowledge of lab techniques but I was equally unimpressed with his total lack of esoteric knowledge, the fundament of alchemy. I was not surprised at a later date to learn that he changed the title of his publication from *Alchemical Laboratory Bulletin* to *Journal of Parachemy*, which, to his credit, was a more honest approach.

Although the course of study was nearing completion, I felt a need to leave immediately. The undercurrents from the Riedels were quite chilling, though on the surface they were cooly courteous and polite.

Other than my skirmish with the now absent Shreya, I got along very well with all the other students and would truly miss some of them. We did get to spend some time together commiserating about the extreme personalities of our hosts.

I had a problem in that my ride back to Chicago would not be available for a few days. I wanted to catch the next bus out of town, but I did not have the full fare as I was short of funds at the time and unprepared for this change of plans. Charles and Barbara came through for me; and, in a very nice gesture, gave me enough to buy my ticket and enjoy myself along the way. I was very grateful for this kindness as I felt that it was urgent for me to leave immediately.

I went to the main house and told Albertus that I would be leaving that day. He did not respond except for a nod. I walked away in disbelief.

As I packed my bag a few hours later, I remembered that I had left a notebook in the library and I went to fetch it. To my surprise when I got there, there were two formidably large men I had never seen before, in suits, standing, arms crossed in front of their chests, on either side of the room in front of the main bookshelves. Their faces were serious and stern. They stood stiffly, staring into empty space, and did not even look at me as I entered the room, like the Queen's Guard at Buckingham Palace. I knew immediately that they were there because of me, and I was stunned. Albertus must have contacted them, whoever they were, when I told him I was leaving, and asked them to come down and guard the premises from me. Obviously I was not trusted. I presume they thought I might steal (or dematerialize?) their books, or some other dastardly act.

My eyes did a quick sweep of the room. I spotted my notebook and snatched it off the table, quickly leaving the library and the two "suits" behind.

I walked back to my room at a brisk pace. The tactics were getting rather heavy-handed and I wanted to be far gone from this place as swiftly as possible. George was waiting to give me a ride to the bus terminal. We walked to the parking lot quickly, sharing a silence that spoke without words. I took one last look at the headless statue draped with the sheet, and finally understood the full significance of this omen. As we drove by the newly laid asphalt I laughed, hearing in my head, "I don't know why they have to use this driveway. It only gets it dirty".

The trip to the bus station was short, but the lingering tension made the trip seem much longer than it was. All I could think on the way to the station was, "I want to get far away from these nutcakes as fast as possible."

I said goodbye to George and eagerly boarded the bus. It was fairly empty so I easily found a comfortable seat. As I sat down, the tension finally lifted, and I smiled to myself and said, "I did it!" as the bus pulled away from the station and Salt Lake City. It was a great relief.

The trip home left me plenty of time to relive my experiences mentally and emotionally, evoking both laughter and concern. I had just lived through a truly bizarre circus act.

Many years later, Israel Regardie, one time secretary to the notorious Aleister Crowley, called me in Chicago to set up a time for him to fly out and study with me. Regardie had worked with Albertus, and during our conversation Regardie asked me what I thought of him. I told him that I thought Albertus' techniques for plant preparation were superb, but I was not impressed with his knowledge of alchemy. In a tongue-in-cheek manner I also said I had the impression that because of certain personality problems and off-the-wall attitudes, he was kicked off another planet and wound up here, to our detriment.

Regardie laughed and said, "Yes, I think you may be right."

At that time I did not know that Regardie had just had years of going round with Albertus until he finally decided that he had had enough and severed relations with him. At least I was not alone in my observations and evaluation.

When *Herbal Alchemy* was published in 1977, Albertus purchased ten copies.

Messing with the
Time-Space Continuum

The Flower House

The city of Chicago has many large conservatories and parks. Growing up, it became my habit to frequent these beautiful public spaces for relaxation and soaking in the elements.

In the early seventies, I had an apartment not far from Lincoln Park Conservatory. The Conservatory is a fabulous gigantic glass structure of Victorian style, built in the 1890s. It is a "paradise under glass" with exotic plants from all over the planet, even full-sized palm trees.

I always enjoyed strolling through and lingering in the displays such as the fern room, the palm room, the orchid room and the flower show room.

I always visited the *Mimosa pudica*, the "sensitive plant." "Pudica" in its Latin name means shy, bashful or shrinking, describing the way it immediately folds up its leaves when touched, an uncharacteristically fast movement in the plant kingdom.

It is quite remarkable to watch; and, if you are easily amused, as I am, it is a lot of fun. But there was a small fence blocking the plant area from the walkway and a sign that said, "Do not touch the plant."

Of course we all know where that goes. Every time I was there, I looked around to see if I was in sight of anyone.

If the coast was clear, I would jump the fence, tickle the dickens out of the plant, and then jump back over the fence quickly, before I could get caught.

One of my favorite rooms was what I called the flower house. It was the huge display area used for the Conservatory's Spring Flower Show, an extravaganza of sweet, heady scents, and floral forms and colors to delight the eyes.

I couldn't get enough of the amazing fragrances. Just walking into that part of the conservatory transported me to another world. At times I would sit there on a bench for a hour or more, just basking in the fragrant ambience of all the flowers and greenery.

On one occasion, after I had jumped the fence and tickled the mimosa, I noticed a very small snail on a leaf. I am not normally into snails, but for some reason, this one captivated my imagination. It was really cute, with two little eye stalks that pointed my way when it was looking at me, which I thought was really neat. I picked the leaf with the snail on it, gently rolled up the leaf and put it into my large coat pocket. When I got home, I put the snail and leaf with extra leafy material into a large glass jar with some dirt – an improvised terrarium. Over the next few days, when I was near the jar, I would look in and wait for the snail to turn its eye stalks toward me; then, with that sign of recognition, I'd continue on with my business of the moment. And, each time I looked at the makeshift terrarium, I thought of the conservatory, the mimosa and the beautiful scent emanating from the flower house.

At that time I was working with a particular technique given to me by Kriyananda to bridge space and immediately put oneself into the presence of the guru.

I decided to hack the technique to try to combine two different spaces: the flower house and my apartment; more specifically, to put the floral-scented atmosphere of the flower house into the atmosphere of my apartment, a kind of an occult air freshener, if you will.

My hack immediately worked. The apartment filled with the fragrances of multitudes of flowers, and was a real delight. For a few weeks, guests walking into my apartment immediately noticed and remarked about the wonderful scents without any cues from me. I just nodded and did not let on about the whys and wherefores. I was thrilled that the technique worked.

However, after a few weeks, I was awakened one morning by an incredibly putrid smell. I couldn't believe it. The whole apartment smelled like a cesspool or something equally nasty. I checked the bathroom first, and then on to the other rooms to try to find the source of the chokingly rank air. I walked out to the back porch to see if it was coming from outside, but the outdoor air was quite fresh without a trace of odor. I went back inside, sniffed about and looked some more, but could not find anything I could trace the smell to. It seemed to permeate every room equally. It was very unpleasant and I was even gagging a bit as I sat down on the couch bewildered, trying to figure out what was happening. After a few minutes of dumb silence I realized it was coming from the flower house!

I figured out what had happened. The flower show was over. I was smelling the rotting dregs of decaying plant material in pots partly filled with stagnant water in the flower house.

I put on my coat and was quickly out the door to see if my insight was true or not. It was a fifteen minute bus ride to the conservatory. I catapulted out of the bus when it arrived at Lincoln Park. When I entered the flower house, I was immediately engulfed by the same smell that woke me up in my apartment. The room had hundreds of empty pots filled with decaying plant matter and water.

What I smelled and saw amazed me. I stood there for a minute or so until the heavy odor overcame my tolerance, and I had to leave.

As I stared out of the bus window on the ride home, I tried to logically process what had just happened, and to consider how to avoid such problems in future experiments. Mucking around with time and space was, to say the least, most interesting.

I had connected two separate atmospheric environments into one locale, a remarkable achievement, with the added bonus of a room freshener. However, like Mickey Mouse as the sorcerer's apprentice in Walt Disney's *Fantasia*, my magic brooms got out of control. The devil's in the details, as they say.

My guru had given me a technique intended to create a continuous and stable connection between the two different locales of guru and disciple, in real time. My hack was made without consideration of, one, the ephemeral nature of flower shows, and two, that I really only wanted the fresh floral aromas, not every scent that passed through the air in the flower house. Purposely locking the scents of the flower house into the air of my apartment without discrimination meant that the odors of anything that happened in that part of the conservatory would be perceptible to me, and affect me and anyone else in my apartment. My little trick could have a lot of unintended consequences.

As I got off the bus, and approached the front of my building, I noticed a couple of my friends waiting for me at the door. In my mad dash I had forgotten that I was supposed to do an astrological chart for them. I apologized profusely for the delay and stated that some urgent business had derailed me.

As I climbed the stairs, sorting out my keys with friends tagging behind, I realized that we were probably about to walk into a very stinky situation.

I said nothing about it, opened the door, and as we walked in we were assaulted by the foul fragrance. Hands to noses, I could see that my friends had gotten the flower house scent. One blurted out, "What is that smell?"

I instinctively responded "Oh, it's the drains in the bathroom. They do this from time to time, awful isn't it? I'll fix it, don't worry."

I quickly headed for the bathroom, closed the door and pronounced the mantra to disconnect the time-space link to the flower house air. To my surprise, the smell was suddenly gone. I sniffed the air a few times to be sure it was really gone. It was.

As I came out of the bathroom one of my friends said, "Whatever you did it worked! That smell just stopped."

They did seem to notice that it was a bit odd that the smell had vanished instantly rather than dissipating gradually; but, to my relief, they didn't ask any more questions about it. I was glad of that, because I didn't think they would have understood, even if I offered a lengthy explanation of the truth. Some things are just better left unsaid.

The unintended consequences of my experiment provided me with plenty of food for thought, bringing to mind classic science fiction mishaps with the transporter in *Star Trek* or the teleportation device in *The Fly*. But, my experience was for real.

Years later I related this incident to someone who, laughingly and seriously, said that I should have put a timer on the experiment, and maybe paid attention to the flower show schedule before trying to alter the space-time continuum. There's a reason the words space and time are spoken together in certain contexts.

Indeed, this nifty little experiment was an example of what scientists would call teleportation. In fact, scents are molecules. They have substance. They are physical objects on a small scale. When you smell something in the air, your senses are interacting with molecules, physical matter.

Austrian quantum physicist Anton Zeilinger and others have teleported the quantum states of single atoms for many miles. That is not the same as "transporting" nuclear atoms, as in my experiment, but, it is on the right track. Science is getting closer and closer to what yogis have been doing for thousands of years without requiring investments of billions of dollars. Just a little bit of knowledge, belief, effort, discipline and time is the key.

But, yogis would not say they "teleported" the physical matter to its destination at all, but that it was there all the time. All that happened was that our awareness connected with it in a particular time segment. As the *Visvasara Tantra* says, "What is here is there. What is not here is nowhere".

Your Aura Is Showing

I have long had an interest in auras and Kirlian photography. As a young adult, I seriously set out to develop my latent psychic abilities. I sought out and read as many books as I could find on the subject. While there were not nearly as many of these books available then as there are now, there were a few, many of which discussed auras and how to see them, and included all kinds of color illustrations and instructions.

I had never seen an aura, and from what I was reading at the time it seemed that this was what being psychic was all about. So, I diligently studied and practiced the various techniques presented in the books I had. After some time, I was able, to some degree, to discern a kind of haze around people's bodies; but I was never confident that what I was seeing was an aura and not just a trick of the light, or distortion from the physiology of my eyes. I never saw any colors, either, in said haze.

I became rather impatient pursuing this path without much to show for it, and realized I did not want to have to spend ten years to develop my aura-seeing capabilities. I really felt that I should be able to get at least some unambiguous results right away.

This was all long before the internet, so information that was off-the beaten track could be quite hard to come by. What we did have in those days, however, was *Fate Magazine*.

Fate was my link to a different world and told me, among other things, that there are other people out there who are interested in the same strange things that I was interested in. In *Fate*, all manner of psychic phenomena were presented in interesting (and sometimes not-so-interesting) articles, accompanied by ads for strange devices such as motor-driven hypno disks, dowsing rods, pendulums; and a vast array of learning opportunities offered by mystical training schools. The ads were sometimes more interesting than the articles.

I welcomed the arrival of each new issue in the mail, settling into a comfortable chair to enjoy a little journey into other-worldly experiences and tales.

One of the ads that caught my attention was for a device called "Aura Goggles." The ad stated that with these goggles and a little effort, you could definitely see auras.

I was, of course, intrigued because I had gone through a bevy of techniques to see auras, to no avail. However, in those days I had to watch every penny I had, and the goggles were not cheap. I gave them careful consideration over the course of several weeks, and finally did mail my check for aura goggles with pinacyanole bromide (a dye) filters.

I was quite excited when I received the package, and put them on as soon as I could get them out of the box. They felt a bit strange, but not too bad. They looked exactly like what pilots in an open-cockpit airplane wore in the early days of aviation.

So there I was, goggles on my head and ready to go! Everything had a violet purple cast from the dye sandwiched between two lenses in each eye frame. When I looked at people, I could see a very distinct haze surrounding them in certain lighting situations. I spent a lot of time experimenting with different people and lighting. It was intriguing for a while, but I became bored with it as I could not see other colors, just a slight purple haze and that was it.

The goggles fell into disuse and were put away.

Some years later at my guru Kriyananda's temple, I was in the hallway, along with some other folks, waiting for him to arrive. As always, I had questions for him about one thing or another. As he entered the temple and began to walk down the hall towards us, he looked very intently at the right side of my body; not at the body itself, but maybe five inches or so from the edge of my physical body. He scanned my right side up and down with concern; then, said "Hello," and went into his office without saying another word.

I didn't get to talk with him that day, but he communicated a lot just by looking at my aura. Several days before, I had given myself a hernia lifting a container at work that was far too heavy for me. I immediately knew what had happened, and was not happy with myself for being so stupid. I knew I should have asked someone else to help me with it.

When I saw Kriyananda that day in the hallway, I realized that he was looking at the hernia injury as shown by its effect on my aura. This was my first experience with seeing auras, except that it was by proxy. I wasn't the one doing the seeing, but I got to see someone seeing something in my aura, something that I knew was there, and that was not otherwise visible. Believe it or not, this was just as satisfying to me as seeing an aura directly myself – a little roundabout, but close enough.

During this same period I received a call from an old acquaintance who wanted to get together for lunch. As I walked up to the door of the restaurant where we were to meet, I saw him coming down the street.

As he walked toward me, I noticed something very strange. He was surrounded by what looked like a black haze. I knew instantly that I was seeing his aura.

Now this person was always troubled and vexed, as if someone had dumped a jar of hornets on his head. He had a tendency to create negative situations by his own bad behavior towards people. I was hesitant when he proposed we meet for lunch, because we really did not have much in common. I felt sorry for him, but I also knew it would be a long time before he changed his ways and figured out it was his bad attitude that was causing most of his misfortune.

Still, I was quite surprised to actually see that black cloud around him.

As he approached, he gave a curt "Hello!" and we entered the restaurant.

All through lunch he was obviously extremely disturbed about something, but he would not talk about what it was. Instead he complained about everything and everybody, displaying a very bad attitude. There was no justification for it either. He simply wanted to be mean.

It was easy to match his behavior and vibe with the black aura I saw around him outside the restaurant.

I was relieved when lunch was over and we parted ways. On the way home I realized that in all the reading and study I had done, I had never found any mention of black auras. There were discussions of dark, murky and swirling colors, but never black. Whew!

My next direct vision of an aura came many years later. A neighbor dropped by, and as we sat and talked I saw that same very dark black haze, as if he had a cloud of charcoal dust around his body. This cloud actually somewhat obscured the objects immediately around him. It was quite remarkable. At the time I did not know much about him except that he definitely had a drinking problem and seemed to be a bit off-kilter. I later found out that this person was known to talk to inanimate objects and yell at them. A lot.

These were the two only times I have ever seen an aura.

At the time I started experimenting with the aura goggles, I had also begun working with meditation techniques given to me by Kriyananda, and it wasn't long before all sorts of phenomena began to occur.

Curiously enough, there was one ongoing development that I paid little attention to, and failed to connect with auras. I was becoming more sensitive and aware of other people's presence and intentions.

Even though this may seem quite obvious, I assumed that I was just getting very good at intellectually sussing out what was before me in a very Sherlock Holmsian manner: analysis, deduction, induction – logic! I assumed I was reading visual cues, analyzing speech, and so forth – quite a conventional process.

But I eventually realized that there was something else going on with this skill, and that there might be more going on with aura reading than visual contact and seeing colors.

For example...

Take the A Train

We needed to get downtown fast. Our pace was quick going into the L station. We burst through the doors to the platform, paid the ticket clerk and tried to move quickly through the rush hour crowd; but, our progress was slowed on the stairway up to the L platform by a dense pack of commuters on their way to work.

About midway up the stairs leading to the platform I had an instant recognition that someone close behind us was intently following us with their eyes, and that they wanted to reach us and do us great harm.

I was absolutely certain of what I was feeling. I had no doubt whatsoever that we needed to immediately maneuver up the stairs as fast as possible to escape being assaulted for some unknown reason.

I knew that it was one person stalking us, and even though there were crowds of people moving up that stairway, I knew that this person had singled us out and had us locked in his sights like a drone ready to fire its missile at us. The feeling was scary and downright disturbing, and I knew in a flash that we needed to move quickly in order to stay out of harm's way; and, we must not look back and reveal to our would-be attacker that we suspected anything.

Still facing straight ahead as we mounted the stairs, I leaned slightly toward Lisa and quietly told her to keep looking forward as we climbed the stairs.

"There's a really bad-news person behind us and something is seriously wrong."

I was concerned that even if we simply turned our faces toward each other as I spoke to her, it would cue this person that we were aware of him, which would put us at a disadvantage.

I then told her that we had to get to the top of the platform as fast as possible; and then, at the top of the platform she should stay really close to me and follow me through the crowd to the part of the platform most distant from the entrance.

Fortunately Lisa had had enough experience with my premonitions to not question what I was saying, and she followed my instructions to the T. She realized there was serious danger.

Like clockwork we quickly threaded our way through the crowd to get to the end of the platform. Once there, I felt we had a safe amount of space and people between him and us, and I told her that it was OK to turn around and see who or what was stalking us.

As we turned to look toward the platform entrance, we both immediately spotted him.

Coming toward us like a raging bull was a tall fellow with a medium build. Hate and anger streamed like laser beams from his eyes – and it was all aimed at us.

We crossed the platform. A train was just coming in, so we moved toward its doors as if we were going to get on. Our would-be assailant was still watching us with fiercely angry eyes, and he entered the train in the next car. As he went through the doors and eye contact was broken, we did an about-face and scurried to the other side of the platform where a train headed in the opposite direction was pulling in. When the train stopped, we were at a door, ready to board.

Our would-be assailant noticed our manuever and got off the first train, but as he tried to cross the platform to our train, he was struggling against the tide of the crowd that was still boarding the first train.

It was a very tense situation. We quickly entered the second train, wishing hard for it to leave immediately. Fortunately, it did, as it was headed away from downtown and did not take on many passengers at this point; so we were away from the platform before the crazy guy could board.

As we pulled away, Lisa and I turned to each other in disbelief! That guy was loco-crazy, insane, mad! Just the look on the guy's face could freeze water and make ice cubes.

It took quite a few minutes for the adrenalin rush to subside, but then I happened to look up at our train's designator flag. It said, "A Train." Strains of Duke Ellington, "You MUST take the A Train.." floated through my mind.

That's how I learned that it's not necessary to see auras, they can be felt as well. If you can feel them, you can tell what's going on without having a person in your visual field, at whatever level, physical or astral. If their consciousness is directed toward you in some way, no matter where they are, you can tune in fairly easily and read their aura, particularly as it pertains to you.

After all those years of trying to see auras, I had learned to feel them. I threw away the aura goggles and never looked back.

So I have been talking about individual human auras, but we can also be strongly affected by group auras that form around incidents of shared experience.

Group Auras

The apartment was really nice, and shared by several young women. It was a walk-up and included the entire ground floor of a handsome brick building with high iron gates at the front and back. Once inside, it had the feel of a fortress, a safe and stable place. Large front room windows looked out toward a beautiful green parkway, a peaceful scene to say the least.

I had just stopped by to visit a friend briefly, but soon after my arrival, various people started popping in. Before I knew it, at least ten people were gathered in the living room talking, laughing, joking and generally having a good time.

About a half hour after I had arrived I began to feel uneasy, which escalated to a deep feeling of dread. Something really bad was happening, but I did not know what.

It seemed to fill the atmosphere of the room I was in, and to my perceptions, it was so thick you could cut it with a knife.

I looked around the room, but it appeared that no one else there had this same feeling. Conversations continued, people laughed and peanuts were swallowed with abandon after being scooped up from little green bowls dispersed throughout the room.

Then, one of my friends not engaged in conversation with anyone, turned on the TV to listen to the evening news.

I couldn't see the screen from where I was standing, on the other side of the room, but I could see her eyes widen immensely as she jumped from the couch to turn the volume up. Everyone in the room turned toward the malevolent box to register their irritation at being so rudely drowned out by the sound.

The news anchor was agitated and read the news haltingly from the cue monitors. Seven young women were found murdered, right there in Chicago, apparently attacked by someone with a knife. All of the victims were student nurses who shared an apartment. It was a gruesome and savage attack, and authorities did not yet know who committed the crime. The perpetrator was still at large!

Everyone in the room was stunned at the report. There was dead silence for a while as we all tried to assimilate what we had just heard. In the silence I realized that the feeling of dread I felt just before the TV was turned on, was a wave of energy – fear and horror – an avalanche of emotion let loose from thousands of people as they heard about the murders on the evening news.

I was horrified by the event, but also fascinated that I had felt a group aura, the mass reaction to the event, before I intellectually knew what had happened.

I learned that emotional reactions shape the aura at the etheric level, and these emotions are contagious. They can be transmitted from one person to another, depending upon the receiver's receptivity at any given time and the intensity of the emotions involved. The strength of the fields of emotion is amplified in groups emoting together in space-time.

Whether you think you're psychic or not, everyone constantly picks up such feelings from auras. This faculty becomes useful when you're able to discriminate; that is, you're aware of your own emotional and thought processes, and you can recognize what's coming from outside yourself.

Sunday Night Blues

Some group aura events are cyclic and color the land-scape with the feeling of the moment. For years and years we had noticed that on Sundays in our neighborhood there is a general overlay of depressive emotional energy. It was quite puzzling because Sundays for us are like any other day of the week, yet nearly always, depression would be in the air on that particular day. We finally figured out that it was the general mass aura of many unhappy people, possibly hung-over from Saturday night, not happy about going back to work or school on Monday, or, having time to reflect on themselves and life in general, they were quite disappointed and did not have the wherewithal to find the grace of the moment. Some people go to religious services on Sundays that raise the specter of the consequences of a life not well-led, and bring to mind their shortcomings and regrets.

Until recently we didn't know that "Sunday neurosis," (also known as "Sunday night blues") was a term coined in 1946 by an Austrian psychotherapist to describe this psycho-logical/sociological phenomenon.

However, we did realize that we were feeling a group aura. Such auras can affect your mood quite significantly, especially if you are not aware that the feeling is coming from an outside source. Many people just accept the emotion as their own without even thinking about it, and even if it is in-congruent with their situation, it becomes part of their aura, and they contribute, to a certain extent, to the strength of the field of the collective aura. And, little bits of particular emotions that we all have to some degree can come out of latency and be amplified when we accept that same flavor of emotion from external sources into our aura.

It is a psychic contagion or infection, just like catching a cold. Having a cold is never pleasant, but unless your immune system is in very bad shape, it is not life-threatening; though it can be quite annoying and inconvenient.

Your psychic immune system is kept healthy by maintaining a good attitude, a strong prana aura, and learning to discriminate what is you and what is not you. If your aura is weak, you can easily be carried away with a collective aura, momentarily or otherwise.

Collective auras are not necessarily bad things in and of themselves. They can be very positive as well. But whether harmonious or inharmonious, or a mixed bag, the key is the siddhi of discrimination, knowing what is yours and what is coming to you from others. As you learn to make this distinction, you will then able to choose what to let into your aura, and what to keep out.

Generally, everyone you have personal contact with, whether by physical presence or otherwise, affects your aura.

Usually before I meet someone for the first time, I get flooded with imagery, voices, and fragments of thoughts and emotions, all related to the aura of the individual I am about to meet.

During my meeting with a person or afterward, I also get another flood of perceptions related to them. Most of the time it is a petty annoyance, since most peoples' auras are filled with junk, a lot of unsorted mental and emotional debris. It is a good idea to create barriers or *kavach* for protection from the streaming psychic video that ensues. Being wide open is great if you want to play The Amazing Kreskin; however, if you want to lead your own life, uncontrolled psychic flora and fauna is quite bothersome.

In my early days of psychic experimenting, a couple of times I tried to combine my aura with someone else's to find out a little bit about them. The few times I did this, I realized that I had contaminated myself, and I had to do double duty to clear it all out. I was quite sorry I ever did this because for several days thereafter my mind was filled with sights, sounds, thoughts, feelings, and emotions that were definitely not me. It was a cartoon-like existence, from my perspective. People have a lot of weird stuff going on in their heads and in general, you don't want to know about it. Most of us have our own loose cannon or two on deck and it's all we can do to keep those in their place, so we certainly don't want to have to deal with the flotsam and jetsam of others as well.

Kriyananda had many similar stories to tell about his experiences in the process of gaining psychic maturity. His advice from experience was to stay out of people's astral space and respect their privacy. What you need to know for your own well-being will come to you anyway of its own accord.

Heart Chakra Burnout

Lisa was a full time student at the Art Institute of Chicago. I would occasionally accompany her to classes and lectures, as students were allowed to bring guests. I actually spent a lot of time there. The Art Institute included a museum, and was in general a very interesting place to hang out. At that time I was teaching hatha yoga and had a lot of time between classes.

Yoga was not as popular then as it is at present, and I remember one prospective student calling to ask about the classes. About midway in the conversation this person said, "Well, I have always wanted to learn how to make yogurt!"

I was a bit stunned to realize she thought that I was teaching yogurt-making, rather than a class in hatha yoga.

That is how obscure yoga was at the time.

So, I was otherwise unemployed and had a lot of time on my hands. I did, however, enjoy sitting in on classes at the Art Institute, as it helped me to forget the details of my penurious circumstances.

It was the middle of a beautiful day. I wanted to get out of my apartment and enjoy the sunshine and fresh breeze coming off Lake Michigan. As I was deciding what to do, Lisa called from school to ask if I wanted to go to the park and the zoo, since it was such a nice day, which I thought was a great idea.

Lisa needed to talk to one of her teachers and get him to sign something, so she asked me to meet her at the school.

Arriving at the Institute I quickly found my way through the familiar maze of corridors to the door of the classroom where we were to meet.

There was a figure drawing class in session. We entered the room, and a nude model on a pedestal smiled at us, while students peered intently in deep concentration trying to capture the essence of the model's form on their drawing paper. As I walked through the room, which was set up in the round, I suddenly felt a very disturbed vibration coming from the instructor of the class. It was one of those "I intensely do not like you" types of vibration, and he shot a sharp glowering glance at me. His instantly hostile reaction took me aback.

At first I could not understand why someone would be so immediately harsh to someone they did not even know.

While Lisa engaged the instructor in conversation and took care of her business, I gazed over the shoulder of a student watching the trail of pencil strokes and erasures as he developed his idea of what the model's butt should look like. Then it occurred to me that the instructor might have been uneasy because this was a nude figure drawing class, so the openness of other classrooms and instructors at the Institute did not quite apply; or, perhaps this instructor was having difficulty with the general policy of openness in this situation. OK, I sort of understood.

As we left the room I could feel his glare on my back, and it was quite a nasty feeling. I asked Lisa if the teacher said anything to her about me being there uninvited, but he hadn't. As we boarded the bus to go to the park I felt the very intense hatred dropped in my aura by the teacher. This nasty energy was spreading like a wildfire and trying to take over my entire aura. I knew I had to get rid of it immediately.

I considered how to remedy the situation. I thought that if I put this guy into my anahata chakra, that chakra's peaceful venusian vibration would smooth out his aura and any strange issues he might have regarding me. So, I combined his presence with my anahata chakra.

After a minute or so I began to feel a very intense burning sensation in the chakra and realized that this was coming from the immense anger, hatred or whatever you want to call it being generated by this individual. I thought that perhaps after a few more minutes the harmonious energy from my anahata would subdue the inharmonious vibration, and the intense heat would subside. It did not.

At this point it occurred to me that my strategy might not have been such a good idea, and I immediately withdrew his presence from my chakra. It took about twelve to twenty four hours to completely rid myself of the burning sensation, and I was very much relieved when it was totally gone.

The intensity of this person's rancor was quite puzzling. There was really no reason for it.

A few days later, Lisa once again called me from school, and asked me to meet her at the same class. I was hesitant to do so, and tried to make excuses for an alternative meeting place; but, she insisted, so I reluctantly agreed.

As we entered the classroom, the instructor was looking over the shoulder of a student, coaching them. He looked up at us and immediately broke out into the warmest smile imaginable. I almost fell over with amazement. As Lisa spoke with him, he frequently looked over at me, smiling as if I was a long lost friend that he had not seen in many years.

As we left the room I was in a daze. So, putting his aura into my anahata chakra actually had worked, in spades. The radical transformation of his attitude had me pondering this incident for days afterwards.

It was now clear to me, however, that I should never combine someone else's aura with mine again. I felt that it could cause major unpredictable upheavals, at a number of levels – physical, mental and emotional. There are better, safer ways to get the same results.

When you visit other people and don't know it

It's great being popular, but sometimes it's not as much fun as you thought it would be. We all enjoy the limelight now and then; however, there is a point where attention can become quite strange and a bit uncomfortable.

I had just finished teaching a course in astral projection and had made friends with some of the students. One of them, Sarah, had invited me to her home on several occasions, and it was great fun talking with her and her family.

One afternoon while I was working on an astrological chart for a client, the phone rang. It was Sarah, who said laughingly, "What were you doing in my kitchen yesterday?"

Having no idea what she meant, all I could say was "What?"

She said, "You appeared to me in my kitchen."

Sometimes I am a little slow in getting the upshot of conversations. I said, "Do you mean you saw me in your kitchen?"

"Yes, that's what I said."

"Yesterday?"

"Yeah."

I had no idea how to respond and it took a while for me to reply. "You must be mistaken."

"No, no! You were here, clear as day, standing in my kitchen."

I repeated that she must be mistaken.

"You must have had a strong visualization, but it wasn't really me."

She came back with a very powerful, unequivocal, "No! You were right here in my kitchen. What were you up to?"

From the tone of her voice I could tell that she thought I was being coy with her in my denial. I went silent, not knowing what to say.

She was quite convinced and insistent that she saw me. There was no arguing with her.

I wondered what was happening. There could be a number of explanations for this phenomenon. I was a little put off by her strong insistence that I was somewhere that I had no recall of.

She thought that I had projected my etheric body into her kitchen; but the fact was I did not intentionally project into her kitchen; or, I should say that I was not conscious of projecting into her kitchen, if I did.

She was so insistent I had to let it go, and changed the topic of conversation.

Later upon reflection, I thought that possibly I did project my etheric body without knowing it and that is what she saw. But it could have just as well have been her own vivid imagination at work. She had just completed a course in astral projection that I taught. Some students are prone to getting carried away with their own fantasies until they have enough experience to discriminate in the non-physical realms.

It did remind me of another incident that occurred to me a year earlier when someone was supposed to contact me to give me some important information that I needed in a timely manner. As the night wore on, I waited for a telephone call that never happened. I went to bed that night very upset with this person. When I spoke with her the next day, she told me that my face had appeared to her while she was lying in bed, and that I looked very angry.

Apparently, sometime in the night I had involuntarily projected an image of myself to her to convey my anger, but I was not at all aware of what was happening. This incident showed me that strong emotions and feelings can cause projections that we are not conscious of.

Another friend once told me that I had appeared to her wearing a white robe and surrounded by a beautiful golden white light. She said that upon seeing me she was immersed in a feeling of great joy and happiness.

How embarrassing! Embarrassing because her description of my presence seemed way too grand for me, and if I was an entity of such cosmic effulgence, how come I had no idea I was there? I really didn't know what to do with that one either.

Over the years I found that during my meditations, some of my students would see or feel my presence. Deep meditation coupled with concern for my students apparently caused emanations from my astral/etheric body to affect those with whom I was in close contact.

It's not unusual for people to build up psychic images of other people that are totally false. They fabricate a well-developed thought-form from their own ideas and feelings about the other person. Such a thought-form can be quite vivid to the person generating it, but may have little to do with the real attributes and activities of the person who is the object of their attention.

Sometimes it can be quite difficult to discern what is actually happening.

In seances, for instance, mediums are often asked to contact deceased loved ones. What exactly does the medium contact? Is the medium contacting the querent's thoughtforms about the deceased; or, are they actually contacting the deceased, or some astral remnant of the deceased; or...?

I have found through my experiences that there is a lot of room for speculation about this sort of phenomenon.

And speaking of the dearly departed...

Ghosts

The Ancestors Speak

This place began its days well outside the Chicago city limits, but as the city grew, it was soon swallowed up into what is known as the Uptown community. It was an oasis in the middle of the city – 119 acres, calm, serene, with several thousand handsome trees, and a pond and a little island connected with a bridge.

It was so popular that it became the permanent residence of many famous and infamous people who appreciated good digs. The architecture of some of the residences was truly "out of this world." There were pyramids, columned temples, and various fascinating structures, some designed by famous architects, such as Louis Sullivan; and the work of well-known sculptors peppered the grounds.

At one point it was a means for me to pay for my education; and it provided me with a direct education into matters of a more arcane nature. I got to be up close and personal with some of the nation's most famous and wealthy people, surrounded by the best art and design in the world. Most people would die for an opportunity like this but I just took it in stride. I never was much impressed by wealth and fame, and really had no idea of who was in *Who's Who*. To get me up to speed, I was given a list of some of the more well-known residents with a quick one line background.

Here's a sample of the notables on the list:

Jack Johnson - First African-American heavyweight boxing champion

Allen Pinkerton - Famous, and infamous, founder of the Pinkerton Detective Agency

Kate Warne - First female detective. Worked for Pinkerton agency guarding President Lincoln.

Augustus Dickens - Brother of Charles Dickens

Cyrus McCormick - Patent holder for a mechanical reaper, farm equipment magnate.

Now I know what you are thinking: These people died a long time ago! I know, I know, but, don't let that fool you – there is more to the story.

I was working for a security firm – a great job for me, because I was also a student at the time and there was always something that I could fit into my class schedule.

We had the contract to guard the Graceland Cemetery and Arboretum at night.

The assignment was fairly straight-forward and simple, but not very popular with the other guards, who were evidently more uneasy around the deceased than the living, which is odd from a security perspective, if you think about it.

My duty began at nightfall and was to patrol the cemetery in a security vehicle, and make a full circuit every so often to make sure that everything was as it should be.

I would enter the grounds between the two massive obelisk-like stone gate posts that framed the entrance. Once inside, I pushed the two big creaking iron gates closed, and bound them together with a padlock and chain to lock myself in until morning.

To be honest, at first the idea of locking myself into a cemetery for most of the night had me a little on-edge. During my first few circuits around the grounds, I was constantly checking the rear view mirror to see if any ghouls had popped up in the back seat, even though I felt a bit foolish doing it. However, I got used to it and soon began to be more relaxed – except when I had to drive by what we referred to as "The Statue of Death." It was a towering sculpture in bronze, itself about 10 feet tall and standing on a high pedestal next to and looking down on Graceland's main road. Robed and cowled, with an arm raised up across the front of its face, it had the stance that Bela Lugosi, in cape, took when he entered a room as Dracula. The cowl was so deep you could not see the eyes, only darkness, and the raised arm, draped with the cape, covered the rest of the face. In daylight, its presence was eerie; at night, the effect was orders of magnitude more so.

The proper name of this famous statue is "Eternal Silence" by the sculptor Larado Taft. Even though I did eventually get accustomed to it, that statue was always capable of evoking a little shiver from me.

After driving a full circuit, I would park near the front of the cemetery where there was some light from the street, and I would usually study for a little while; then, another circuit. So it went night after night.

I would vary my rounds from time to time and explore, in vehicle and on foot. There was a lot of ground to cover with many interesting areas, and seemingly infinite little byways off the main tracks, full of surprises.

I had favorite spots to visit, such as the Ryerson mausoleum, an Egyptian Revival design by Louis Sullivan. It is a tower with three narrow windows, a mastaba-shaped base, and crowned with a step pyramid; all in large polished blocks of dark grey granite. It was a magnificent structure.

Another Egyptian Revival structure that I really liked was the Schoenhofen mausoleum, a pyramid with a sphinx on one side of the entrance and an angel on the other. The entrance was modeled after the gateways at Karnak in Egypt; and the doors were decorated with bronze lotuses, and had handles with asps coiled around them.

On moonlit nights the cemetery seemed vibrant, the many monuments of white stone glowing in the dark. Graceland is known for its eerie nocturnal ambiance, and was the location for part of the movie *Omen II*.

One of the most haunting images of Graceland is the statue of Inez Clark, a 6 year old, who, as legend has it, died during a thunderstorm. Her grave is marked by a life-size statue in white marble, sculpted with amazing detail. She sits with a hint of a smile, on a rustic chair, holding a parasol and a flower. Her circa 1880 dress is trimmed with ruffles and eyelets, all meticulously carved out of the white stone, as is her ribbon bedecked hat, locket and bow-buckled shoes. The whole statue is enclosed in a glass case.

Seen in the light of a full moon, it feels as if the stone is about to come to life, and indeed there are stories of that happening down through the years. I was told that one guard became so spooked by the statue of Inez that he rushed out of the cemetery and refused to go back.

On one bright full-moon night I was walking through a section of very old, low profile stone markers. I spotted what appeared to be a hole with something white sticking out of it. It glowed in the moonlight. As I approached, I thought it looked like a skeleton's hand, but I told myself that my imagination was getting carried away. But, I approached the hole, bent down to investigate, and sure enough, it was what I thought it was. I stared at the hand for a few minutes trying to figure out what had happened here. Obviously ground heaving had compromised the old wooden coffin, and lifted its contents to the surface. At any rate, the person buried here was making themself known and perhaps trying to make a break for it, I chuckled to myself.

The living may tend to fear the dead, but Graceland is also home to dead who fear the living. George Pullman was a very wealthy railway magnate who became quite hated when he lowered his employees' salaries while raising their working hours and rents. The resulting 1894 strike was bitter and violent, with 34 of his striking employees killed by federal troops.

Upon his death just three years later, Pullman was buried at night, in a casket lined with lead, and surrounded by several layers of concrete and asphalt, reinforced with steel rails – all in fear of very angry people who might try to dig him up and desecrate his body.

Spending nights in a cemetery is not the first choice of things to do for most people, but it does have its benefits. As a budding Tantric I could appreciate this situation in light of the traditional Tantric practice of meditating in charnel grounds at night. In such a place, you are confronted with the impermanence of it all, and you start thinking about the larger issues in your life. As a meditation practice it flushes the bats out of the belfry and helps to clear up the mind. To some degree it brings us to face to face with our selves, our fears and our ersatz bogymen. Confronted with them, we have an opportunity to transcend them and transform them into constructive energy.

One night on my rounds, I began to ponder ancestor worship as I looked at the tombstones surrounding me.

According to Chinese folklore, we have what could be called several souls. One tradition is that astral humans consist of hun and po. At death, the hun goes to a heavenly sort of realm, and the po resides close to the earth realm. The living provide a spirit tablet to contain the po of the deceased, and this is kept on an altar in the home. The living descendants burn incense daily and talk to their ancestors through the spirit tablets, telling them the latest news and asking for help in earthly matters. Traditions vary in their details, but the practices are quite similar from region to region.

I decided to test this concept. It seemed to me that I should be able to contact my own ancestors, if there really is something there to contact. As I drove through the cemetery, I called upon my ancestors to contact me and to give me a sign. I repeated this request many times in my mind. I was quite serious and truly expected my ancestors to show me a sign in recognition of my request.

I drove through the cemetery for the next hour or two, constantly on the lookout for something to appear before me. At one point I was startled by a large tumbling ball of weeds blowing across the road in the wind. Occasionally dust devils swept up leaves in a small tornado and moved down the road in front of me.

But, as the night wore on, and I observed nothing remarkable, I completely forgot about contacting my ancestors, and was no longer watching for signs. My attention was elsewhere.

On one of my circuits I marveled at the bright moonlight and the beautiful shadows it created on the ground, the crisp clear outlines of many tree limbs. It was a work of art! I turned the vehicle toward an area that I called "high ground" as it had a slightly higher elevation than the rest of the cemetery. On a whim, I got out of the car and started walking this portion of the cemetery, which I had never done before.

It was as if I were being drawn to this place. As I moved between rows of tombstones I was suddenly stopped. My body turned to the right, where there was, directly in front of me, a tombstone. In the light of the full moon I could easily read the inscription – Hurley – my own name!!!!!

I stared, unable to think, my body totally still.

After a minute of two, I regained my composure and began to smile and laugh. I really did get a timely, no-nonsense response to my request for contact from my ancestors. This experience was an eye opener in more ways than one. What the mechanisms of this event were, I don't really know. It could be interpreted in a plethora of ways. I have a hard time believing that the spirits of the dead are just hanging around, waiting for us to try to contact them; but I surely did get a response, where ever it came from.

The Man with No Face

At the end of each month renter's blues would hit. We would be reminded that we had to pay a huge amount of money for the privilege of another month of having habitable space in the city of Chicago; and that money would turn into vapor, with no promise of getting ahead a little bit in the future. As I put the check to the landlord into the envelope, I felt dismal about ever being able to get off the renter's treadmill. Once and a while we were able to save up a little bit; but then the rent would go up or something else would happen to make us bleed money.

Of course I was only in my twenties, and this state of finances was not unusual for my age group. At that time it was a massive undertaking to pull together enough assets for the sizable down payment needed to buy a house.

Contemplating the situation with a bottle of very cheap wine, we concluded that we needed to act to improve prospects for the future. The problem was we did not have any extra money to invest. But, being mentally resourceful and having plenty of pens from work and lots of brown paper bags to write on, I did the math and developed a strategy to manage this endeavor. It seemed that with some lifestyle tweaking – for instance, fasting a few days a week and then eating minimally, and avoiding spending on entertainment or any other frills – we could possible make this work. Well, perhaps it wasn't really that bad, but the situation called for a tight budget for sure.

So, the plan. We would buy a two-flat house and rent one flat to pay the larger portion of the mortgage on the house, insurance, taxes, repairs, and so forth. It would still require a good portion of our earnings from work to cover costs, but at least we would be suffering for a future in the sun rather than looking down the long dark tunnel of endless rent payments.

I launched myself into action and personally visited a number of real estate agents each week. The idea was to get to know each agent and their staff well enough to comfortably elicit information about properties on the market that other people might miss in their real estate search. There were bargains to be had, but you had to keep close to the action, have good connections and pay close attention to get in on the game.

After several months, my diligence paid off. I received a call from Bob, one of the agents I had been checking in with.

"I think I have just what you are looking for. Very nice neighborhood, a low down payment, and a tenant already in one of the flats. The building is in sterling condition and it's being offered for a price you cannot refuse."

He said he could meet us there in an hour. When we arrived at the address given, I was quite impressed with the outside appearance of the building, and the general ambiance of the neighborhood with its well-manicured lawns and many large trees. We walked up the front stairway and rang the bell to see if Bob had arrived. We were a bit early and did not really expect him to be there yet, but the door opened and there he was.

"How do you like it so far?"

"The outside of the building looks great, and the neighborhood is really nice."

"Well, wait till you see the inside and the backyard."

We moved through the house quickly as Bob directed our attention to all the fine points. He then asked if we would like to meet the tenant on the second floor. We were a little hesitant, but decided to anyway.

We rang the outside bell for the flat and were buzzed in. As we ascended the stairs I noticed how remarkably clean and well-kept everything was.

We were greeted at the second floor landing by a kindly, gentle, yet vacant-looking woman who appeared to be in a daze. She had a constant smile on her face as we walked through the flat, but she was also pensive, as if she had something she desperately wanted to say but could not or would not.

One of the rooms of her flat was totally occupied by dolls. It had a large couch with dolls lined up on it from one end to the other. Dolls also sat on or stood on the floor and sat on chairs. It felt a bit strange, as for me, dolls have a kind of sinister quality at times, especially in large numbers. Along with the tenant's subtle pensive demeanor, the upstairs apartment was giving me an uneasy feeling.

After a quick tour we shook hands, all smiles, and Sheila, Bob and I descended the stairs back to the ground floor flat.

I looked around and took in more detail. The cleanliness of the place was quite impressive. That we liked. But I noticed that the basement floor was freshly painted, which seemed odd; and, one of the dining room doors dragged tightly over the carpet. The carpet was brand new and did not yield to the door readily, as it would if it had seen some use.

I asked Bob if this was new carpeting. He immediately said, "No."

His reaction was abrupt and struck me as odd, but I let it go and moved on to look at the rest of this immaculate house.

"Well," said Bob, "What do you think?"

He gave us the figures and said that the absentee owners would work around any difficulties we might have to finalize the purchase of the building. The eagerness to please was surprising given the price, condition and location of the place, which were such that one would expect the property to be swept up very quickly.

As we walked down the stairs I thanked Bob for his time and efforts and said we would call him in a few days to let him know if we were going to make the purchase.

Sheila and I looked at each other as we walked away from the building.

I spoke first. "You know, this is really strange. Did you notice how hard it was to open that door with that carpet in the way. It had to be a new carpet, don't you think?"

"Definitely just installed," she said.

"And the basement was immaculate, with the newly painted floor…" I added.

Sheila looked over to me with a slight frown and said "Those dolls with the woman upstairs were really freaky."

"Yeah, that room reminded me of one of those horror movies where the dolls come alive when you're not watching."

We looked at each other, both thinking without saying, "Something is squirrelly with that place."

That night we talked about the too-good-to-be-true real estate and decided that we definitely needed more details. For instance, where was the owner? Why was one of the flats empty? Why was there obviously new carpeting which the real estate agent insisted was not new? Why was the basement just painted? Why was the woman upstairs acting so strangely?

That night as the lights went out, the events of the day slowly drifted away into the deep space of sleep. After several hours I was suddenly awakened by Sheila's voice. She was sitting up in bed, peering around the room intently, and seemingly deep in thought about something. She didn't even notice me rolling over.

"What happened?" I said.

"Uh, I was asleep, I rolled over and my arm banged against something by the side of the bed and woke me up."

"What was it?" I said.

"When I opened my eyes there was a man standing right next to the bed in his BVDs."

Yikes! I scanned the room instantly at those words and got up to see if the door was locked. No one was in the room and everything was secure.

"Weird dream you had."

"No, it wasn't a dream. He was here right next to the bed and I banged him with my arm when I turned over. But when I looked to see who it was, I saw that half of his face was missing. It just wasn't there."

Sheila knew enough so that if she said it was not a dream, then I knew it was not a dream, it was some sort of apparition.

"How strange," I said, "a ghost in his BVDs. You would think he could at least dress up before going out at night."

We both laughed went back to bed.

The next morning over breakfast we talked about the strange apparition, but that was forgotten as our conversation turned to the flat and the strange circumstances there. We decided to investigate on our own since it did not seem like the real estate agent would come forward with any enlightening information for us. He had definitely lied and was uncomfortable about the carpet; and was overly eager to sell the house at a bargain basement price.

We decided to go door to door down the block to ask neighbors if they knew anything about the former occupants, owner, or the house. It was a rather brazen thing to do, but we felt compelled to.

We arrived in the neighborhood early in the afternoon and began knocking on doors and talking with neighbors.

Nobody seemed to really know anything, or perhaps they didn't want to talk about it. But then we hit the jackpot.

At a two-story brick building across the street and about five houses down, a middle-aged woman in an apron answered the door. We introduced ourselves and said that we were considering buying the house in question and wondered if she knew anything about the former owner or the house.

With eyebrows raised she stared at us for what seemed an awfully long time, but was probably only a few seconds. She glanced down at the floor and then her eyes directly fixed on mine and she invited us in for some tea. We were thrilled.

We sat and waited in suspenseful silence, eager for the revelations to come, as she laid out cups, saucers and cookies and waited for the water to boil.

After pouring the tea, she sat down and looked at us.

"Do you know anything at all about the house or the owner?" she asked.

"No. Nothing at all."

"Well, about six months ago I was sitting in the living room and noticed several police cars and an ambulance outside the house you're asking about. I walked down the block and across the street to find out what was going on. I asked one of the police officers in charge if he could tell me what was happening. He said that the owner had died, but it was quite a while before anyone knew he had died. The owner had four cats as pets, and the cats, when they ran out of cat food, fed on the dead body of the owner. They ate part of his face."

Both of us were stunned. I felt like my body had turned into marble. The ghost without a face!

We sat immobile until I collected myself enough to continue the conversation.

We thanked the woman profusely for this information. She said that she was glad to be of service, and, after finishing our tea, we left, smiling nervously.

As we walked down the street back toward the house I could not help but think of the East Indian stories of *skondhokata bhoots*. These are people who lost their heads one way or another and became ghosts, constantly searching for their missing heads, and often pleading with the living for assistance. In our case, however, it was a semi-faceless ghost telling us what the real estate agent did not want us to know.

As we walked past the house on our way home, I looked up at the second floor windows with their lace curtains and wondered how soon it would be before someone bought the house. With the mystery solved we had decided that renting was not so bad after all. Further real estate adventures could wait for a long time!

Ghosts in a Pickup Truck

At one time I thought it would be a great idea to connect up with some genuine ghosts to see what was happening on the other side. One night before I fell asleep I asked for some ghosts to visit me. After falling asleep I had a remarkably vivid dream of a young couple in a pickup truck.

They said "Hi! So, you want to see some ghosts?"

I looked at them quizzically.

The guy in the pickup truck said, "Well, we're ghosts."

Both smiled mischievously as he said that, and then they both laughed.

The next thing I knew, I was flying through the air, som-ersaulted and landed on my knees beside my bed.

I was quite awake by now.

At first I had thought I was somersaulting in my very vivid dream, but as my aerial adventure continued, I realized it was a physical event. I was catapulted out of the bed, ex-ecuted a full somersault in the air and skillfully landed on my knees. When I hit the floor it took a while for me to gather my wits as I looked around the room. There was nobody in the room except me. I mused on the fact that I had just been flipped out of my bed by two prankster ghosts.

I decided that the next time I do this — if there ever was a next time — I would be certain to put qualifiers on what type of ghosts I want to see and what I want them to do. Enough of this riff-raff. I did not really appreciate becoming an acro-batic projectile at someone else's whim.

I told a friend about this incident the next day, and she smiled wryly.

"Oh yeah, I have the same ghosts, only they take over my body and make me go to the refrigerator and eat ice cream in the middle of the night."

OK, she didn't believe my story.

Anyway my advice is that if you ever have the urge to call in ghosts, put well-thought-out qualifiers into your request, or get references, as there are pranksters out there.

Materialization

The Golden Chain

It was a typical Chicago heat wave with no relief in sight. There was not even the slightest hint of a cooling breeze coming off Lake Michigan.

I arrived at the branch library uncharacteristically early because it was too hot to sleep, and headed downstairs for the lockers and break room.

My fellow library workers, like me, were mostly marking time until better employment could be found, and pretty much kept to themselves. The library's necessary enforced quiet did not lend itself to an atmosphere of camaraderie and socializing, anyway.

My job was not challenging, but it was not unpleasant and helped to pay the rent. I re-shelved books and kept the stacks clean and orderly. I silently pushed a rolling book-shelf between the shelves, finding the proper Dewey decimal address for each returned volume.

Well, it was a boring job, so I developed ways to relieve the monotony. For instance, when I found myself in the neighborhood of topics that interested me, I would pause and page through a book or two.

The other way I amused myself was by materializing various scents in the stacks and then watching the response of library patrons: quizzical looks, sniffing the air and wondering where the delightful scent came from. But, even that became routine and I decided I needed a new endeavor to liven up my workday.

Gold! I had just re-shelved a book on gold panning, which gave me an idea: I would try my hand at materializing gold.

Why not? After all, I could materialize scents, which are, in fact, solid matter, so why not something a little more dense? Gold!

For the next hour and a half I meditated on materializing gold as I shelved books.

After closing time, I and my fellow workers passed quickly through the basement locker room with no banter, just a lot of quick movements. Everyone was out of there in a flash.

It was a short walk home from the library. As I began to relax into a leisurely pace, I noticed something on the sidewalk. It glistened in the sun, long, twisted and snakelike – it reminded me of kundalini. I bent down to take a closer look and discovered it was a beautiful gold chain. It was broken, and must have fallen off someone's neck as they were walking. It was quite long, hefty, and of very good quality gold. I picked it up, and as I let it slither from hand to hand, I realized that this was the gold I had asked for!

It was not exactly the Kohinoor diamond, but I was very impressed as I had never found anything like that before.

Coincidence? Yes, people lose things all the time and other people find them all the time, but...

I had asked for gold to come to me, and in a matter of a couple of hours, here was gold in my hands.

In hindsight it is remarkable that I did not pursue gold materialization any further at that point. I like gold and I am not averse to monetary gain, so you would think that I would ramp up my efforts and aim for intact jewelry, hefty ingots or golden bejeweled idols. But, for me, the process, the magic of materializing is what makes my juices flow. The fruits of my efforts are only of passing interest.

Because the gold I found was someone else's loss, this incident brought to mind Sri Yukteswar's story about Afzal Khan, written about in Paramahansa Yogananda's *Autobiography of a Yogi*. Afzal Khan was a fakir who, in his youth, was given certain siddhis in return for his kindness of fetching water for a yogi. One of these siddhis was to be able to summon a genii named Hazrat. Hazrat could spirit away anything that Afzal touched.

Later in life, Afzal went to the dark side and let his greed get the better of him. He would visit jewelry sellers and ask to examine their wares, feigning an intent to purchase. But, what he was really doing was touching various pieces so that after he left the shop he could have Hazrat spirit away the jewelry to be rematerialized into Afzal's possession.

Eventually Afzal's activities came to the attention of his benefactor, the yogi that gave him the power to summon Hazrat. The yogi, disguised and baiting him with gold, caught Afzal in the act, called him the Bengal terror, and promptly took away his powers.

I had no designs on other people's possessions and was not comfortable that my good fortune was someone else's misfortune. I pondered the present incident and wondered if in a past lifetime I had lost a gold chain, and the person who lost the gold chain this time around found my gold chain in a previous incarnation, and…. Egad! This sort of thinking could make you crazy. As I continued my walk home, my thoughts about ethics and causes gave way to the sensation of the heavy gold chain in my hand.

Gold! Hazrat, are you there?

A Good Thing Becomes a Not-So-Good Thing

You wouldn't believe how some not-so-normal things become normal, and when they do become normal things, you react to them in a much more discriminating way than you previously would have ever thought possible.

It never occurred to me that my new-found siddhis would not always get rave reviews. However I found out that, as with everything else in life, one needs to balance and control one's efforts.

Lisa was well acquainted with my experimental yogi self and more or less accustomed to the phenomenon surrounding me. One very sunny day we decided to go for a walk. As we descended the stairs and ambled on to the sidewalk I decided to materialize rose incense in the air surrounding us. Immediately the scent appeared out of nowhere, and, as we walked, the cloud of scent became thicker and thicker. Soon it became overwhelming and I started to cough, but did not dematerialize it as I was feeling very smug that I was able to get such a powerful and thick materialization. However, Lisa also began to cough and gag on the heavy scent.

Suddenly she blurted out, "Could you turn that down a little? It's a bit too thick and I'm choking on it."

A little embarrassed, I dematerialized the scent and brought things back to normal. A minute later most of the scent was gone, except for a trace lingering in my hair. As we walked on we laughed about it – yes, there certainly can be too much of a good thing.

A few days later Lisa suggested we visit her brother as she had to drop something off. It was a short bus ride to her parents' high-rise apartment where her brother was living. The doorman was all smiles and super courteous, opening the doors and pushing the elevator buttons. Lisa's parents were quite well-to-do, so much so that I felt rather uncomfortable every time I went there. I really was not used to having people push elevator buttons and open doors for me.

As the elevator ascended I imagined what it would be like to get used to this sort of life-style. It sent a shudder up my spine. I was wondering what the doorman was really thinking behind his paid-for smile.

As we exited the elevator Lisa mentioned that her parents were away for a few days. I grinned because Lisa had a key and we were welcome to raid their refrigerator. They had what I considered the best of everything when it came to food.

Approaching the door, we could hear the sound of an electronic synthesizer. Dave, her brother was home and busily tweaking circuits on his electronic instrument. At the time, synthesizers were very new and experimental. All three of us were enthusiastic about the brave new world of electronic sounds, so we had a lot to talk about as we raided the refrigerator and discussed our mutual interest.

Dave let me play with his synthesizer for a while; then, during a lull as I was trying to figure out how to make a particular sound, he said, "Lisa said you could materialize scents."

I was a little surprised since I didn't know that Lisa had mentioned this to him. I paused, wondering how to respond, since for most people, such things are too far out to comprehend. I didn't know where he was going to go with this.

He then asked if I would materialize a scent for him. He said he was skeptical, but that he had an open mind, especially after hearing what Lisa told him. He considered his sister to be a very practical person, and not given to imagining strange things.

After getting over my initial surprise at his request, I sat on the floor in padmasana position and had him join me by sitting on the floor in front of me so that we faced each other. After he settled in, I asked him what scent he would like to have materialized. He chose rose incense.

In a few seconds we were surrounded by the very strong scent of rose incense. He looked at me in utter astonishment and was speechless for a few seconds. Then, he blurted out, "You are a really good hypnotist!"

It certainly was not a response I expected to hear, and I didn't know how to react.

He sat there for a few minutes, sniffing the air with a confused look on his face as the scent slowly faded away.

I realized he had put himself in a compromising position, unwittingly. He did indeed have an open mind, but he also always gave his rational mind the upper hand; so, he needed a rational explanation for every phenomenon, lest his world view (which did not permit the reality of materialization to even get to the starting gate) be totally undermined. This event blew a fuse in his logic circuits.

He very quickly let the moment go and was on to other things. But, his demeanor was changed and revealed unsureness with every movement he made and everything he said, as if he was still trying desperately to place the experience within his psychological comfort zone.

Lisa and I left soon afterwards without giving the incident much immediate thought; but over the years I have often pondered Dave's reaction, especially in the face of similar reactions from other people – and there have been many.

A Goddess Visits

One night I was reading about various gods and goddesses in the Hindu pantheon and I decided to try a particular meditation technique to see if I could catch a glimpse of one of these deities. I chose the goddess Kali.

I practiced the technique for about half an hour, but did not see anything. Then, as I slowly opened my eyes to end the meditation, I saw before me a shimmering image of a very beautiful woman. At first it was wavy, undulating and a little faint, but then slowly it became solid, stable and in full color. I knew instinctively that this was Kali, as I had asked for. The vivid image hung in the air before me for about fifteen seconds and then dissolved in the same way that it had appeared. My meditation had precipitated a very unusual materialization, by a renowned visitor. I felt most honored.

Visual materialization of any sort is always very interesting to see. One night I awoke for no apparent reason. I opened my eyes and saw someone who was sleeping in the same room, get up and sit at the edge of the bed. I got up and asked my friend if they were OK. As I did this, I saw that their physical body was sound asleep, lying in the bed and I was talking to their etheric double. I leaned forward to touch the double and as my hand reached for it, it vanished. I looked at my sleeping friend, wondering whether or not they would be aware in the morning of the fact that they had projected.

Akasha —
If You Try Sometimes, You Get What You Want

It was not easy to get face time with my guru. He was constantly on the move, always busy at one thing or another. His appointment book seemed to always be filled up, and I had to resort to ambushing him from behind potted plants, or cornering him on elevators and stairwells.

In our relationship I felt like a latchkey child, left home alone with a key to the house, some bread, peanut butter and jelly and a note about what to do in case of emergency.

Still, it was OK with me, as that's how I grew up. I was used to the routine and accustomed to being left to my own devices most of the time.

On one occasion I was lucky enough to bag him for a few minutes and grill him for the answers to some questions that seemed very important to me at the time.

Kriyananda could be a real smart-ass at times, and this rude aspect of his personality grated against me. But, he was who he was, and I was who I was. Ultimately that all was of little importance in the scheme of things because I recognized that he had knowledge and skills that I wanted. He was my guru. I simply adapted and applied work-arounds in order to communicate and wrench whatever information I could from him, and then run for cover before he figured out that I just snipped a lot of time out of his busy schedule.

On one occasion I jumped him as he was entering his office, and made my plea for a scrap of his time to further my spiritual development.

He gave me an exasperated look, stared down at the floor briefly in thought, then looked up and said, "OK. Five minutes!"

Smiling, I followed him into the office and took a seat in the huge chair in front of his desk. As he sat down, he looked at me disinterestedly.

I waited attentively for a cue to speak. His eyebrows went up, he thrust his head forward. I quickly translated this as a "Whaddya want, let's get this over with" look.

I began to tell him about my latest meditations and magical experiments. At that time I was beginning to work with an akasha mantra he had given me. I wanted to ask him about his experiences with that same mantra so I could get an idea of what to expect. I asked him.

He took a long look at me and said, "Try it and find out for yourself."

I told you he was a smart-ass.

He shrugged and continued, "Do japa with the akasha mantra until you discover what you want to know." (Japa is mantra repetition.)

My first thought was, "God! What a punk guru I have."

Astrologically he was a double Taurean with a big shot of Virgo on the side. Of course I was inclined to be annoyed by his stolid practicality (all that earth element) since I am seventy percent air and things can never happen fast enough for me.

But, I knew that, underneath it all, he was, in fact, really concerned about teaching me well.

One of his most frequent sayings was the old saw, "Give someone a fish and they will eat for a day, teach them how to fish and they will eat forever," or, translated, "Get off your ass and do some work and you will own it but if you just ask and I give you the answers you will never own it and in a sense I would be doing you a disservice."

Now, what I have just said is one possible interpretation of this incident. Another was simply that I really annoyed him and he just wanted to get rid of me as quickly as possible.

Either way, I was left to do japa on my own, and it did work out quite well, really!

As the first part of my efforts to understand and experience the element akasha, I decided to chant the akasha mantra all day as I went about my business. I would only stop doing it when I had to speak to someone, or had to think about something that could not wait.

I was spending the day with Lisa, so I told her about my project so that she'd understand my strange behavior.

It started off as a warm pleasant day with a nice breeze coming off the lake, so we decided to walk from downtown to our north side destination rather than take the bus.

About an hour into our walk I noticed the breeze was no longer coming off the lake. I was beginning to feel quite hot and was perspiring profusely. It broke my concentration with the akasha mantra, and I muttered offhandedly to Lisa, "You know, I could really go for a cold Coke right now."

Before Lisa could even respond to this, a woman burst out the door of a store front, arm outstretched and aimed directly at me with a can of cold, unopened Coke in her hand.

She looked me straight in the eye and said "Here, you drink it. I pressed the wrong damn button on the soda machine."

Amazed, I caught the can as she thrust it at me, and before I could get out, "Gee, thanks!" she had stormed off as abruptly as she had appeared.

Lisa and I looked at each other and laughed.

We continued our walk, but now with a little refreshment. I mused about how different people would describe this event. Some people would call this coincidence, or serendipity, or synchronicity.

I was working with the akasha element, which has no time or space to slow down the results of thought, so sometimes it can instantly materialize objects and events from thought. Since I was constantly repeating the akasha mantra, I presumed to define the event as a moment of magic. I was thrilled with that thought, as it was exactly what would be expected from the element akasha as I had been taught.

After getting over the novelty of that moment, I dutifully resumed my silent chanting of the akasha mantra as we continued our walk. Along the way, my japa was interrupted with the thought that I needed a dresser with drawers, a night stand, and a desk for the apartment I had just moved into. The thought vanished quickly as I brought myself back to the mantra.

Several minutes later two men cut across our path on the sidewalk carrying furniture out of an apartment building onto a moving van.

Lisa recognized one of the men as her cousin. "Hi Rick!"

He looked up at her and smiled, "Hi, how you doin'?!"

He put down the chairs he was carrying. "Moving day, I just rented a new apartment."

He paused for a second and then said, "Either of you want a dresser, a desk, and a night stand? I have too much furniture for my new apartment and I need to get rid of these."

I immediately said, "Sure, I could use them!"

He even offered to drop them off at my apartment on the way to his new apartment. Coincidence? Serendipity? Synchronicity?

No, no, no. Magic, I think.

The next time I saw Kriyananda, I said, "Very interesting, this business with the akasha mantra."

He responded with a knowing smile and raised eyebrows, but before he could even begin to speak, I said, "I've got some other questions for you..."

So you want to be psychic

"Now this book looks practical.. detailed, sensible techniques.. I think I could work with this."

With those comments to myself I scooped up *How To
Make ESP Work For You* by Harold Sherman. I paid the
clerk, tucked it into my pocket and was on my way to becoming PSYCHIC!

Back home, I dived into it and was half way through the
book in one sitting. The next day I finished the book and
was ready to apply Sherman's technique.

I sat down in a comfortable chair and visualized a white
movie screen in front of me with my eyes closed, as directed
in the book. I kept my attention on the screen and watched
for the images that were supposed to form on it. Except for
hints of a couple of cartoon-like figures, I saw nothing. My
screen was blank and stayed blank.

I followed up with another exercise: I would stare at the
imagined blank screen, ask questions and wait for a response
to appear as an image on the screen. It was a bit like using a
Ouija board without the Ouija board.

I stuck with the screen techniques for days, which turned
into weeks, then, finally, at the end of a month with no suc-
cess, I gave up. For some reason my white screen wanted to
remain blank and not cooperate at all. Seemed liked there was
no one in the projection room or working the projector.

I continued reading lots of other books about psychics
and psychic phenomenon. Over a short period of time I had

gathered a small bookshelf's worth of really interesting experiences that other people had had; and several methods in detail for achieving supernormal states of consciousness. I even got a Ouija board, but it only talked nonsense to me, and I already had plenty of that in my life.

Eventually I accumulated some serious texts on esoteric disciplines, found a guru and began to meditate. I had more or less stopped trying to be psychic and was concentrating on simply discovering the universe.

TV Psychic

One evening I sat down for my routine meditation and went into a very deep state quite quickly. I was enjoying the peace and relaxation of the moment, when, out of nowhere, a deep voice broke the silence, "MURDER INCORPO-RATED!"

"What the... ? What is that, and where is that voice coming from?" I opened my eyes but there was no one to be seen in the room nor the apartment. I was rather unnerved. I had sat down to meditate and experience peace of mind and I get "MURDER INCORPORATED."

"My god," I thought to myself, "I must be a lot sicker in the head than I ever thought I could be."

We all have deep dark thoughts now and then, but this was way out of proportion. It was a very loud and robust voice and it had gruesome overtones – not what I would expect or want when sitting for meditation.

The experience was disturbing and it took me a while to calm down. I stood up and shook my head back and forth as if to shake the strange (and I thought demonic) voice out of my cranial vault. This was not the kind of content I wanted rolling around in my brain.

I sat back down after gathering my wits and bravely decided to try to meditate again. I was a little hesitant, but I was also determined not to let whatever it was ruin my meditation. As I slipped into a deep meditation state, I felt more at ease and comfortable; but, then after a half a minute it happened again: "MURDER INCORPORATED" in a loud, firm voice in my head.

"Holy mackerel, I must be going bonkers!" I got up immediately with my eyes wide open. "This is not good," I said to myself.

I was getting freaked out and decided to watch TV to divert my mind from what had just happened. I went into the living room and turned on the TV. As I walked toward the couch I was again physically trying to shake the voice out of my head. I was also glancing around the room somewhat frantically, hoping to anchor myself in some rational explanation of any sort, some kind of proof that there were no murderous demons inside my brain.

The first words I heard from the TV were, "MURDER INCORPORATED." It was the David Susskind show. I watched with rapt attention as David Susskind interviewed a guest who claimed to be a former member of the infamous Murder Incorporated.

I was astounded. I was tuning in to TV in my meditation! A psychic TV guide. This was amazing, but most of all, I was very, very relieved to know that I was not going bonkers. I was just picking up TV broadcasts. Without a TV.

Now this does not much resemble the siddhis mentioned in Patanjali's *Yoga Sutras*, but this capability was a fruit of my meditation practice, and an indicator of increasing psychic awareness.

Of course I asked myself, what exactly was I picking up?

Was I actually receiving a TV frequency and translating it into something about the program, in my consciousness? In "real time"? Was I having precognition of what I would hear when I turned on the TV? The odd thing was I was getting nothing about the conversation itself or the people involved, but instead, a sort of announcement made by a very distinctive voice which did not belong to the interviewer or his guest.

So, a psychic TV guide? Great! All of this effort and work to meditate to expand my consciousness and I get TV programming! What happened to the blissful oceans of light?

Weeks later I was meditating in the late afternoon and again heard the same deep voice, but this time it said, "DENBY!"

I got up, opened my eyes wide as I could, and shook my head, just as before. Then I resumed my meditation position, and heard the loud, firm voice repeat, "DENBY!"

I immediately thought of the *Murder Incorporated* incident, so I got up and turned on the TV. For about a half hour I cycled through channel after channel but found nothing that seemed to relate to Denby.

Several evenings later I happened to get engrossed in a TV movie about a woman who was kidnapped and buried alive. It was a cliff-hanger where her husband was trying desperately to find her before she ran out of air. As the clock was ticking off her last minutes, the husband found a clue to her whereabouts. The name of the town she was buried in, and… it was DENBY!

So, my psychic TV guide had not failed me after all – it just gave me the programming several days ahead of time. I reflected that my wish to be psychic was granted, but… TV blurbs?

These two experiences got me to thinking about how, in the modern world, our minds are constantly bombarded by radio and television broadcast waves. That catchy tune that pops up unprompted in your head may not just be an access of your memory banks, but could be you picking up a broadcast from a radio or TV station directly.

The conversion of electromagnetic waves to audible sound by the human body and mind is a scientific fact and called electrophonic hearing, or the Frey effect, named after Allan H. Frey who experimented with the phenomenon in the early 1960s. He and other scientists transmitted modulated voices on microwave frequencies and found that people in the path of the transmitted radiation could hear the voices as audible sounds in their head, with no receiving equipment of any sort.

So, have you been hearing voices in your head lately?

During World War II, Lucille Ball (*I Love Lucy*) was picking up radio stations on a temporary dental filling. She also noticed a strange Morse code transmission in a specific area along her daily commute. She reported it to the FBI, who quickly investigated and found a transmitter and a spy at the location where she was hearing the Morse code in her head.

Still, I don't think what I experienced was me picking up electromagnetic waves directly because I was getting a sort of synopsis in a phrase or word; and, in the case of "Denby," what I heard was not heard at the time of the broadcast.

So, why television programs, and why these particular television programs? Perhaps it was because both had strongly emotional content and dealt with intense subjects. The particular vibrational frequency and strength of this emotional content was probably able to penetrate into my consciousness at the time.

Over the years, I have had plenty of other voice experiences. For instance, I notice that often after I engage in a conversation with someone during the day, later, when I settle down for the night to sleep I get a lot of chatter coming from their mind and from the various entities (embodied and not embodied) surrounding them. This can be quite annoying. Sometimes it starts several days before the encounter, and can persist for days afterward. I have learned to apply special techniques given to me by my guru to get rid of the chatter.

I also frequently hear voices from astral traces of deceased relatives and god knows who else. I usually just shove them out, because I've noticed that relatives and other such types are usually just as stupid dead as they where when they were alive (think of all those horrific Thanksgiving and Christmas get-togethers). I feel sorry for those who seek the advice of the dearly departed because they usually don't know their yin from their yang. Being dead does not confer wisdom – it only confers physical death! Besides, what mediums contact is just as likely to be the querent's thought-forms about the deceased as the actual deceased person.

As my psychic faculties have developed, I have come to realize that most of what goes on in our heads, or, more specifically, goes through our heads, does not originate with us but comes from external sources, such as the thoughts of other people in our environment, or people that we are mentally or emotionally connected to, not to mention human media permeating the airwaves.

Now, when someone asks me how they can become psychic, I reply, "EMPTY YOUR MIND AND MEDITATE ON NOTHING." If you practice this at least daily, you will become quite psychic in a matter of a few months. If nothing else, you may be able to know what is on TV without the bother of electronic equipment.

X-Ray Vision

I was feeling particularly good and was extremely eager to work with a newly-learned kundalini technique. I lay down in bed to meditate, and a few minutes after I had closed my eyes, an image began to form. I was seeing a series of thin boards in front of me within the ceiling. Between the slats was mold, and I presumed that since I was living in a top floor apartment, that the moisture from the flat roof had seeped in and created the moldy condition around the wood plaster slats. After a while I was satisfied that I had seen enough of moldy slats and decided to open my eyes and see if the x-ray vision would linger. I opened my eyes quickly and found the ceiling as usual, a very smooth plaster and no slats were visible.

I lay there for a while wondering if indeed there were plaster slats in the ceiling. How could I find out, short of tearing the ceiling down? As I gazed upward, the light in the room changed slightly and I noticed dust lines running across the ceiling at the same distance as the slats. Here, in faint outline, was proof that I actually did see the moldy slats.

For the next few days I was quite entranced by this experience of x-ray vision. What was happening was that I was seeing with my etheric eyes at just the wavelength where I could see through the dense plaster completely. I found out in later experiments that I could more or less control the degree that I could see through an object. Normal eyesight is limited to quite a narrow band of perception; but, by raising my consciousness to a higher vibration I could see right through dense, slower-vibration material objects.

By the Pricking of My Thumbs
Something Wicked this Way Comes

It has been said that just because you're paranoid does not mean that they're not out to get you.

Relaxing at home one quiet afternoon on my day off, I was gazing at the floor when a clear image appeared to my mind's eye. There were five women gathered around a heavy, round wooden table, having a scheduled meeting to discuss what to do… about me!

It seemed my presence was inconvenient for their plans, and they intended to get me out of the way. The meeting was called specifically to discuss particulars and strategies in regard to getting rid of me!

I knew who these people were and where they were, but I could not understand why they wanted me "out of the way."

They knew of me, but none of these people had ever met or spoken to me.

No part of this psychic vision made any sense to me. I thought I must be going off the deep end. There was no logical reason for such a nefarious plot.

Despite my misgivings about the reality of what I was seeing, I could not shake the feeling that what I saw was indeed happening, and at the moment that I saw it.

At the time I was in one of those fill-in-the-cracks relationships that gives you something to do while waiting for the more substantial parts of your life to come by, and Sandy worked with the people, and at the place in my vision.

That evening I told her about the experience. She listened thoughtfully, but other than raising her eyebrows, she had no comment on my revelation; and I suspect that she was thinking that I was slightly delusional.

A year and a half passed, and Sandy and I went our separate ways. Later we were speaking on the phone tying up some loose ends, and she said, "Oh, by the way, you know that time you said that there was a meeting of women at a round table, discussing how to get rid of you?"

I thought for a second and said yes.

"Well, you were right, it actually happened, just like you said.

" Some of the women at work wanted me to date this fellow they had in mind for me, and, as a matter of fact, I found out that I was hired for this job because they thought I would be the perfect match for him. When they found out about you shortly after I was hired, they held a meeting around large round wooden table in this room at work. They were discussing at length how they could break up our relation-ship and get me into situations where I would be working closely with the fellow they wanted me to date. Then, they actually scheduled work sessions and tasks that would throw us together.

"I was unaware of all this scheming until today, when Martha, who had been at the meeting, told me about it."

I couldn't help but feel smug at this revelation, but that was tempered as I also relived the truly creepy feeling that I had when I originally remotely witnessed this incident. Fact is truly often stranger than fiction, and here was yet another example of how nutsy and meddling people can be – way beyond what is considered normal, rational behavior.

I trusted the vision enough to be on my guard in relation to certain people and events, and I emerged unscathed from that episode in my life.

Getting confirmation of this incident showed me the power of siddhis. I was becoming privy to a lot of informa-tion that is not available to others; but, I had to develop new ways to deal with this additional input and find practi-cal ways to navigate the often-treacherous labyrinth of other peoples' agendas.

This demonstrated for me conclusively that the world is frequently not at all what it seems to be, not that I had any doubts on that account.

Psychokinesis

Other people influence our lives more than most people think. The average person who does not practice meditation usually has a hard time separating outside psychic influences from their own thoughts and emotions. Most people believe that whatever they think, feel or do is a product of their own will.

Those who go deeply into spiritual discipline learn that there are many psychic forces at work, including those generated by other people who want to influence events to promote their own agendas.

The extent to which psychic force can affect physical matter is astounding. The etheric body or *pranamaya kosha* (prana body) is the medium for most psychokinetic phenomena; and there are many people without any "spiritual training" who instinctively know how to work with this energy to affect other people's etheric bodies.

One of the strongest occurrences of psychokinesis that I have ever experienced was when I was staying at a friend's house for an extended period of time while I was in transition from one living situation to another.

One Sunday I decided to attend a lecture a few towns away. I got into my car and took off down the road for a pleasant drive.

A few miles along in my journey, my arms and hands wanted to steer me off the road! It was as if they had a mind of their own. The muscles in my hands tried to move to swerve the car, but I fought the physical impulse and kept it on the road. I felt this strongly several times. It was quite unnerving to say the least, very real and very forceful.

After about five minutes of this struggle, I pulled off to the side of the road. Several mantras later, I cautiously continued on my way. The rest of the trip was uneventful.

When I returned home that evening, I sat down to contemplate the day's events. Obviously whoever was trying to control my driving did not wish me well.

I remembered a story Kriyananda, my guru, told me about an experience he had in his formative years of becoming a yogi. He was visiting a yogi acquaintance, and they were talking about various siddhis.

Kriyananda asked the yogi to show him an example of a siddhi that he had acquired. The yogi was obliging. He got up and stood at a window, and beckoned my guru to come. The room they were in was several floors up and the window looked over a bustling street with stop lights and lots of traffic. The yogi pointed out a pedestrian waiting for the light to change so that they could cross the street.

He told Kriyananda, "When the light changes and they walk to about the middle of the street, I am going to make their eyelids close."

The yogi waited, and then as the pedestrian crossed the street, the yogi made a motion with his hand and fingers, as if he were closing their eyelids. Kriyananda saw the pedestrian immediately launch into total panic, spinning around and flailing their arms. It was obvious that something had suddenly happened to them – they could not see where they were.

Then, the yogi made a motion with this hands and fingers as if he were raising their eyelids. Instantly, the pedestrian stopped spinning and flailing, and resumed crossing the street, disappearing into the crowd.

Needless to say, Kriyananda was quite impressed, but he had been expecting something a little more tame and was uncomfortable that, in a way, by asking for a demonstration, he was responsible for the pedestrian's fear and panic. But, it left him no doubt that one person can physically affect another person at a distance.

My driving experience reminded me of that story.

A few weeks later the same phenomenon occurred again. It was a milder, but strong enough for me to realize that someone somewhere was trying to control my body movement.

Still, it was not the first time I knew I was intentionally being affected physically from a distance.

On one occasion I was riding home on the bus, blankly staring out the window. Suddenly I felt someone's hand reach into my chandra chakra (where the skull meets the back of the neck) and twist it around as if they were trying to break it or just generally trash me. I immediately recognized who was doing this, and put a stop to it. I was really disturbed, and when I got home, I immediately telephoned the person responsible. He answered the phone, and the first words out of my mouth were, "What the hell do you think you are doing?"

He knew exactly what I was talking about, and apologized profusely for the malfeasance. His explanation was he had phoned me, but he was frustrated that I was not home, and in a little fit of anger he had etherically grabbed my chandra chakra. Not a good idea...

A Vise of Ectoplasm

Lisa walked into the dining room where I was studying and said she was seeing and feeling very thick energy engulfing her. As I looked at her I saw a kind of haze surrounding her with two clamps poised as if they were a vise around her head.

She said she was getting a head-ache from it, and I could see she was beginning to panic. I knew that I had to draw the energy off and away from her, which I did immediately. As soon as I pulled the etheric globule off her head, she said that she felt better.

It still hung in the air, visible as a subtle but thick haze which both of us could see. It was also tactile with kind of a plastic consistency when we reached out to it with our fingers.

I pointed a knife at the vise and commanded it to dissolve, making cutting motions through it in the space that it occupied in the room. It diminished in size gradually, and after about fifteen minutes had totally disappeared.

It was what mediums refer to as ectoplasm, a sort of etheric bioplasma with weight and substance. Both of us knew right away from whom the manifestation had come, and we had to figure out how to respond.

This particular person thought it was amusing to prank us in this manner. We had excused prior incursions as over-zealous experiments, but this one had a decidedly deadly edge to it. Other incidents were rather aggressive as well, but for some reason, we, shall we say, forgave him his trespasses.

However, this time he had gone too far, and we had moved beyond being mildly annoyed to being outright aggravated. Lisa and I decided that retribution was called for.

It just so happened that the perpetrator who aimed this rather vicious thought form at us, had just purchased a house and was in the process of moving into it. We decided that I would haunt his newly acquired house to teach him a lesson about civility and proper psychic etiquette.

Several days had passed since the vise incident and it felt like the proper time to send him a message. I sat down to meditate and moved into a deep trance state. From this depth of trance, if the time is right, one can easily influence events at a distance.

I projected my etheric body to his newly acquired residence and began to open and shut doors, make strange sounds and other sorts of Halloweenish mayhem. After a half an hour or so of this, I came back to my body, opened my eyes, smiled at Lisa and gave her the high five. We both laughed about it for days.

We had no immediate feedback about my efforts as his phone had not yet been connected, so we had to wait until he contacted us. A couple of weeks after the incident, we received a phone call from the miscreant.

I asked him how his new house was working out, and he blurted, "That house was haunted! I was in there cleaning up when suddenly doors started opening and closing and all sorts of other strange things began to happen."

He went on and on about the haunting and I had all I could do to hold the laughter in. I laughed so hard at one point that I had to put down the phone and cover the mouthpiece so that he could not hear the guffaws.

But, what he said next quelled the laughter. He said that he couldn't stay in the house at all and had immediately put it back on the market, and was looking for another house.

In a sense we felt a little sorry for him, but then again, people who think that other human beings exist merely for their personal amusement and power games tend to rack up unpleasant karma. He was a nice guy in many ways, but at times was rather misguided and could be dangerous if not reigned in. He needed a better understanding of the repercussions of wielding his considerable natural psychic abilities, in other words, some sort of spiritual discipline and consciousness of ethics.

Hopefully, he learned something from this incident.

Water and Etheric Energy

Human etheric energy, or prana body, as yogis call it, interacts with the prana of other people, places and things.

The prana of a place is formed by the particular way the four elemental energies – earth, water, fire and air – configure at that location. These energies accumulate and dissipate, their flow affected by the natural and man-made features of the place, among other things. The art of understanding these elemental energy flows is called feng shui in Chinese culture and vastu in East Indian culture.

Water is of special interest for yogis and other psychically sensitive people, who have always understood the usefulness of the magnetic qualities of flowing water to soak up and dispel disturbances in one's etheric body and the etheric environment.

Kriyananda often recommended turning on a faucet to get rid of disturbing energy; and taking a shower or bath each evening with the conscious intent to clear out any inharmonious vibrations accumulated during the day. He also suggested taking walks by streams, rivers and waterfalls for the same purpose.

Water dowsing is a good illustration of the effects of water's magnetism on the etheric body. When the etheric body of a receptive person such as a dowser feels a vein of water, the effect on the etheric body is sufficient to move a physical object, such as a divining rod, held in their hands.

Paul Sevigny, former president of the American Society of Dowsers, would occasionally give demonstrations of water witching at the ASD's annual convention. The first time I attended, I got to experience the phenomenon directly.

There was a platform for a stage erected outdoors with a vein of running water in the ground beneath it. For neophyte and would-be dowsers, Paul would have volunteers come up to the stage to try out their dowsing capabilities. He would show them how to hold their dowsing rods, and have them walk across the platform, over the vein of water and see if they got a response. Some did and some didn't.

I walked across the platform and over the water, but got nothing from the rod. Paul walked up to me, put a hand on one of my shoulders and had me try it again. As I walked across the stage, he walked with me, his hand on my shoulder. When we came to the spot where the vein of water was, the dowsing rod nearly ripped itself out of my hands, pointing down forcefully toward the underground water.

It was an astonishing feeling, as though there was an invisible hand pulling the rod downward.

Since that time I have acquired numerous sorts of dowsing rods and occasionally polish one up and take it for a walk. Sometimes I am good at it, but most of the time, not so good. I certainly would not want to have to depend on my dowsing skills to find anything, but it's an interesting practice.

The Spinner

Early in my studies with my guru, he suggested that to learn to work with prana/etheric energy, I make a little spinner – a piece of paper folded into a sort of pyramid shape, balanced on an upright needle set in a wood base. I constructed the device and set it up on a dresser in my bedroom.

I stood about ten feet away from it and directed it to turn left. To my surprise, the spinner started turning left. I then commanded the spinner to stop. It immediately stopped. This was too easy! Even though I built the thing, I didn't expect it to work for me so readily. I had anticipated many hours of effort and concentration to get any results.

I commanded it to spin right, and it spun right. I then commended it to stop and spin in the opposite direction. The wheel stopped immediately and began to spin in the opposite direction. I spent an hour and a half playing delightedly with the spinner. Off and on for the following several days I would play with the spinner, and demonstrate the effect to anyone in the vicinity. But, after a while, the novelty wore thin and I was on to other things.

About a month later I went back to it, and set up the needle and spinner to try again. I got decent results but not nearly as crisp and definitive as my first attempts, although the megba was still there, more or less.

I never really put much practice into working with it, but every few years I bring it out to try my luck. Sometimes it works, and some times it doesn't. I suppose if I practiced with it regularly I could get more consistent results, but like so many other things on my to-do list, it has fallen by the wayside.

The Parting of the Ways

There have been occasions when I have gotten definite psychokinetic results with very little effort

Many years ago, a friend and I were walking down the street on our way to meet some other people. It was rather cold out and we were walking briskly. Ahead of us were two people walking quite slowly and I knew that we would overcome them quickly. They were each quite large, and walking together abreast, they took up the total width of the sidewalk.

I was considering how to ask them to let us pass by them without sounding rude. They were unaware of us approaching from behind as their attention was directed ahead of them, and the soft snow made our footsteps silent. As the distance between them and us closed in to about ten feet, I made a gesture as though I was pulling a pair of window curtains apart. As I did, the two men abruptly separated from each other on the sidewalk, leaving a clear space in the center for us to walk through, which we did.

Why I did that and why it worked, I do not know. It was an instinctive act with no thinking involved, simply a hand gesture.

I have experienced may different instances of the physical nature of etheric/prana energy and its effects but this next one stands out as one of the most curious.

The Case of the Sexy Blouse

Sheila was, to say the least, very gregarious and full of surprises. One evening she burst through the front door of our apartment with a mischievous gleam in her eye.

"You won't believe this, but I just met the neighbor who lives upstairs. She was wearing this blouse that was absolutely oozing sexual energy, I mean, I've never seen anything like it before!" and she went on and on about the blouse.

Although I found it very interesting, I really didn't know how to respond to this one.

Suddenly Sheila blurted out, "I know! I'll go up and ask her to take it off so I can bring it downstairs and you can feel what I'm talking about."

"What the.. ?" I was still trying to formulate a response and wondering what on earth was going to happen next; but before I could get any words out of my mouth, Sheila dashed out of the door and up the stairs to the neighbors' to ask this woman she had just barely met to take off her blouse and loan it to her so that she could bring it downstairs for me to feel.

Really! This is a true story!

Sheila soon came bounding down the stairs, sexy blouse in hand.

"Oh my god!" I thought. "She actually got this woman to take off her blouse so that I could feel it up."

Bewildered, I watched as Sheila thrust the blouse into my hands, and, with a wide eyed giggle, awaited my response.

I have to say, I could feel very strong sensual energy from the blouse before it even hit my hands. In my hands, it pulsed with sex vibe. All I could say was, "Whoa!"

I fondled the silky fabric with delight, and both of us started laughing.

The blouse was literally dripping with strong sexual energy.

"If we could bottle this, we would become millionaires," I joked.

After several minutes of fondling and comments, I gave the blouse back to Sheila so that she could return it to its owner. As she went out the door I was smiling, and shaking my head.

This was the first time I had ever felt an object so powerfully impregnated with prana, and I then realized what strong energy generators humans are at times, impregnating our clothing and the objects around us with our thoughts, feelings, emotions, bio-energy, etc. Anyway, this object lesson, in my opinion, was a great way to learn about such things.

Sex Vibe at a Distance

As every Tantric knows, sexual energy is a potent accumulation of etheric bio-energy, and other people can feel it. This is no astounding revelation. But, not so many people realize that sexual energy can be felt unhampered by distance.

Sheila and I had recently met a couple, Andy and Michelle, who stopped by one morning to visit us on their way to the beach for a day of sun and surf. We both noticed that the two of them, how shall I say, were overflowing with a sensual and sexual vibe.

They stayed briefly and then departed. Later that evening, we were sitting and chatting when I suddenly felt this wave of sexual energy inundate my aura. I looked quizzically at Sheila, and before I could say anything, she looked at me and said "Yeah, I noticed it, too."

I said "I think that energy is coming from Michelle and Andy."

"I think you're right."

"I think they are having…"

"Sex," she finished my sentence.

The vibe was quite intense for about ten to fifteen minutes, then it slowly diminished. So, why did we feel this energy in particular? Was it a general broadcast of energy? If that were the case, I would think that everyone in Chicago would have been lit up and been walking around with... a smile on their face. Perhaps we were part of Michelle and Andy's fantasy play. And, maybe because we had recently been in physical contact with them, in other words, in their auras, we were simply sensitive to their activities. I don't know the answer to the question, as it would have been a bit tacky to ask them what they were thinking about when they were having at it that night, and as it turned out, we never saw them again.

My experiences have been a formidable series of lessons about how certain energies, subtle and not-so subtle, affect us and others. I have learned that we are all a part of an enormous interactive energy system, for good or ill. Some vibrations are toxic and some are pleasant. Some are not directly harmful but are annoying. Bio-energy, vital energy, etheric energy, prana, chi (whatever you wish to call it) can be used to heal and soothe and protect ourselves and others, but it also has a darker, destructive side. It is important to learn to discriminate and choose whether to filter out or allow particular energies into our systems.

The ability to perceive these energies and their characteristics is tremendously helpful for anyone trying to understand the real driving forces behind the surface of events. It is a necessary part of our ongoing education as we expand our consciousness and awareness, and hopefully become more skillful at the art of living.

The Cat's Meow

Sensitivity to the ebbs and flows of etheric and other energy is not limited to homo sapiens, but exists in other species as well.

For instance, many people are aware that their pets, or shall I say, our other-species companions, can also be sensitive to energy fields.

Amber was a pleasant and playful fluffy ginger tabby cat, and normally not much into vocalizing. However, every time anyone in the house would hit a certain meditative stage (usually five to ten minutes into a meditation session), she would start howling loudly, and go on and on. It was totally disruptive for meditation. We would have to stop meditating and get up in order to get her to quiet down; and, if one tried to resume meditation, she would again commence howling, just as the meditator would enter a strong alpha state. This did not just happen once or twice but nearly every time she was in the house and one of us was meditating.

She did not seem to be picking up physical cues, because she didn't respond to us going to our meditation places and assuming meditative positions. The kitty opera always began later, just as one would enter a deeply relaxed state, wherever she was in the house. She was definitely responding to the energy change.

This got to be quite annoying and really put a damper on attempts to meditate. Meditation time had to be grabbed opportunistically when the cat was outside. It was aggravating, but at the same time it was quite fascinating to learn that other species can be quite aware of our psychic states and respond to them by communicating in their own language.

Books, Libraries and Astral Books

In my study of astrology I learned early on that I was seventy percent air (I have seven planets in air signs), so I am an air head, which explains why I like to read so much.

That I love books is for certain. When I was in grammar school, I would often walk down the street with an open book in my hands, reading intently as I negotiated crossing Chicago streets in a multi-tasking miracle.

Long before the days of the internet, I spent many hours in the Chicago Public Library's central location, a fabulously elegant work of architecture which later became the Chicago Cultural Center. From the time I was eleven, about once a week I would spend nearly the whole day roaming the stacks for new and interesting books. I had many interests, chief among them being science, general do-it-yourself projects and esoteric subjects such as astrology, magic, mysticism.

I was lucky to have access to a resource that could fulfill my inquisitive mind's need for knowledge; and that this resource was also a breath-takingly beautiful place to be.

It was constructed in 1897. Stairways, walls, and pillars were marble inlaid with mosaics of iridescent glass, pearl, and stone; and massive mahogany doors led from one space to another. There were two large Tiffany stained glass dome ceilings, one of which showed the twelve signs of the zodiac. It was a an architectural masterpiece, and had an inspiring ambiance for my introduction to the world of knowledge.

For me, this library was an entity. It was friendly, alive, and it wanted to feed my insatiable curiosity.

I felt secure there and considered it my second home, so much so that people I knew would actually leave me notes tucked into the index file cards in subject matter headings that they knew I was interested in. Considering that there were many hundreds of index card drawers, it was always a treat to find a secret message hidden there just for me.

One day, wandering in the stacks, I involuntarily stopped, as if halted by an invisible hand. I looked to my left, and saw a book about yoga, and then to my right, where I saw a book about hermetics. Both of my arms reached out simultaneously and I plucked both books from the shelves at the same time. In my left hand was *Autobiography of a Yogi* by Paramahansa Yogananda, and in my right was *Initiation into Hermetics* by Franz Bardon.

At that time, I had been reading my way through every esoteric book in the place, devouring them at a frenetic rate. The pickings were getting slim, so these two books with their rich history and profound knowledge were just what I needed. Together, they were the quintessence of my spiritual quest: a fusion of the magic of the East and the magic of the West. I had been desperate to find a clear path that I could count on for results. In my meditation that particular morning I had asked for such help and direction.

Grasping the two books, I sat down right there in the stacks on the glass floor. With great excitement, I thumbed through each of them to absorb as much as I could immediately and get an idea of what they had in store for me.

Initiation Into Hermetics was an unusual find in a public library. It had just been translated from the original German and was quite obscure, not distributed by any major suppliers of books. It was a specialist text that would be of interest to very few people; not something one would expect the average public library to include in their acquisitions.

I believe there was something at work in this case beyond a chance encounter. Something had brought me to those two books at a certain time, and finding them marked a turning point for me. They became the two most important books in my life.

Back home I quickly read through both books within a few days.

Yogananda's well-known autobiography was inspirational and provoked me to look for a teacher. That book led me to my guru. Oddly enough, all I had to do was open the telephone book where I quickly found a listing for Kriya Yoga training, only about four blocks away from the library.

The teacher was Goswami Kriyananda. He was not only an initiate of the Kriya lineage (Yogananda's lineage) but was also a quabbalist, hermetic and a tantric; and preceptor of The College of Occult Sciences and the Temple of Kriya Yoga. His guru, Shellji was a direct disciple of Yogananda, and also trained and initiated in several western occult traditions.

Shellji was a master of getting down to the essence of what really makes things work, be it yoga, quabbala, tantra, or Pennsylvania Dutch hexes. His was an eminently practical approach – a fusion of the knowledge traditions of East and West, yet still connected deeply to the wholeness of these traditions.

Through Kriyananda I was trained in hermetics as well as Kriya yoga, and Tantra kundalini yoga. The perspective of this lineage is that the various techniques of all these disciplines are ultimately based on working with the same source, which is akasha.

My Book Genii

In my astrological studies I later learned that the planet Uranus in my natal chart was positioned directly on the degree in the zodiac related to a genii that brings books to you that you need. Uranus also is the planet that rules electricity and electrical devices like Tesla coils; and kundalini, siddhis, magic and other similar things, so it has always been really easy for me to ask for books about these subjects and quickly be guided to a source for exactly what I needed to read about.

There was a bookstore in Chicago that I occasionally visited which had a collection of rare esoteric books locked in a glass case. I was especially intrigued by several books from the 1500s in this collection. I asked the owner if he would open the case for me so that I could look at them.

He gave me a brief look on his way to the back room, and, nose in the air, said with disdain, "No! You can't afford them."

I was rather hurt and resentful of his attitude, but managed to finish my business there with a smile, trying to cover up the sinking feeling I had from being treated so rudely. I vowed to never again set foot in that store.

Eight years later, I received a phone call from someone asking me if I would be interested in teaching some courses at the bookstore they were about to open. They said they had no money to pay me, because they had just spent it all setting up the store, and buying out the stock of a now defunct bookseller.

I was game. I've never cared about making money from teaching esoterics, and the fellow on the phone seemed pretty nice.

Soon after we met, Sam said he liked me very much and offered me half ownership of the bookstore if I would teach there. This took me by surprise.

"I'm grateful for the offer but I prefer to keep my teaching endeavors independent from my business activities."

He wasn't expecting this response. We both knew that it would be a very good economic opportunity for both of us, so he could not quite fathom my reluctance to engage.

As we spoke, I was helping him unpack boxes of books and shelve them. As I opened one of the boxes, two very old books caught my attention. They were the same two books that I wanted to look at eight years earlier in the glass case.

This was astonishing – now I could touch them and page through them and handle them to my heart's content. I took the books out of the box and showed them to Sam.

"Where did you get these?"

He laughed. "They came with the bookstore I bought out."

He reached over to another box, pulled out a carved wooden sign and put it on the table. The sign was from the very bookstore where I first saw these books.

As I paged through them gently and reverently, Sam noticed my demeanor.

"If you want them, they're yours. I have no use for them."

I was surprised at his statement. "These books are four hundred years old. They've got to be worth a bit of money, to say the least."

But, he did not seem to care at all. He shrugged and repeated what he had said before, "If you want them, they're yours, I have no use for them."

Still in shock, I thanked him and set the books carefully aside for their trip home. As I opened the other boxes and shelved books, I was struck by the irony that the very bookstore that I was in years earlier, where I was snubbed, was now being offered gratis for me to own. And, I was given exactly the books that were previously rudely denied to me.

In addition to bringing books to me, or me to books, the book genii has given me the ability to quickly feel the essence of any book. With a laying-on of hands and a very short perusal, I can give a synopsis of the contents. At times, students have asked for my opinion about various books and what would be valuable for them to read. One such incident occurred in a neighborhood bookstore where I happened to be with a few students. One of them approached me with a book by Bhagwan Rajneesh, later known as Osho.

I looked through the book for about thirty seconds.

"This guy is quite brilliant and has a lot of wonderful insights; however, he is going to get himself in serious trouble because he totally lacks discipline."

I urged my student to study the material in the book with caution. There were important key disciplines omitted that were necessary to be able to engage in and implement Rajneesh's ideas.

Years later, Rajneesh was incarcerated and deported from the U.S., his troubles definitely a result of his serious lack of discipline.

You're Not Crazy

Books can also save us from harm and truly give enlightenment, as one woman discovered in a fortuitous way.

Years ago in one of our favorite esoteric book stores we happened to meet a woman there who asked if we knew anything about kundalini. She then related to us what she called "a most interesting experience."

One night she awoke to find herself in her bedroom walking around. She had no recollection of getting out of bed, but there she was, totally awake and walking around. She thought at first that she had awakened from a sleepwalking episode, though that had never happened to her before. Puzzled, she walked back toward the bed to lie down again. As she approached the bed, she gasped in fright as she saw herself lying on the bed, not moving, her complexion pale and her body lifeless. She thought, "I must be dead!" On thinking that, she immediately was drawn back into her body and opened her physical eyes. She was totally conscious during this whole experience.

This was the first of many out-of-the-body experiences that she had night after night.

Sometimes she would leave her body immediately upon lying down and find herself in other very different worlds, all of which were delightful, but frightening to her, in that she was totally conscious and did not have a clue as to where she was and what was happening. The experiences were as real to her as any other part of daily life; and she began to believe that she was going off the deep end and needed psychiatric or medical intervention.

She thought she would lose her sanity totally if she did not get immediate help. She saw her doctor, who referred her to a psychiatrist and other medical professionals to diagnose and recommend a treatment strategy.

While they conferred over a period of weeks about the possibilities of either shock therapy or drugs or a combination of both, she happened to meet an old friend that she had not seen in many years on a bus ride home. This friend happened to be carrying a book she was reading about kundalini, and she began talking enthusiastically about the phenomenon. As the woman listened she realized that what her friend was describing was exactly the type of experiences she was having.

The next day she bought herself a copy and read the whole book in one sitting. She said that a powerful wave of relief swept over her as she realized that her experiences were a great gift to be enjoyed and not to be feared. She considered herself to be very lucky as she was very close to having treatment that might very well have left her electroshocked or a drugged-out automaton.

As she spoke, we could feel the power of her relief and happiness as she described her discovery of the nature of these mysterious events in her life. This had occurred over a year ago, and since then, whenever she had the opportunity, she would visit the bookstore to see if there were any new books on kundalini and astral projection to add to her already sizable library. She also was able to connect with groups of people who have had similar experiences world-wide. She was a happy person telling her story, and her aura as well as her physical demeanor showed that she was now a content and enthusiastic adventurer, full of life and energy.

This person was very fortunate that circumstances put reading material into her hands that exactly mirrored her experience and saved her from a horrible fate in the clutches of the mental health and medical community. This is not to say that health care providers don't have a place in the scheme of things, but at times they do not know their place in the scheme of things. There is a need for intervention in true cases of mental breakdown, but the western medical tradition is not yet mature enough to understand that there is a difference between hallucinations they might see in cases of maladjusted psyches, and the beneficial real space-time shifts in consciousness that occur as kundalini awakens.

As you can see, I have a deep respect for books. They can heal and enlighten. It truly is a siddhi simply to be literate, able to read and understand.

Astral Books

Physical books are interesting, but there are also astral books. I first ran across them while practicing vajra vidyut many years ago.

After just a few minutes of meditation, I found myself out of my body and out in the astral. In front of me was an elegant book stand about four feet high. On it there was a large book, opened for me to view. As I moved closer to it, I could see that the script written on the pages was beautiful, but one I'd never seen before, and the language was unknown to me.

This was a recurring event in my projections. The books were always magnificent, but I was disappointed every time I saw them because I knew they contained great knowledge and wisdom, but I had no interpreter, and no ability to read them myself. Usually, as I approached the books to try to decipher them, I would be thrown back into my physical body.

But, quite consistently, a few days after a visit to these astral books, I would receive a great piece of knowledge or insight on the physical plane, either from a book, self-realization, or a teacher. What I thought was being denied me in the astral would actually come to me in a physical form.

Years later I was attending one of Kriyananda's lectures, and he mentioned an astral room full of beautiful jewel-encrusted books on stands. He described six books to the right and six to the left if you are standing in the center of the room. Each book represents a sign of the zodiac. They contain the history of every action of the past. The truth of any matter could be known by looking through these books. They were large, but light as a feather; and as you read a page, the following page would appear.

He called this astral experience the akashic records, and explained that this was his symbolic astral experience of akasha.

I found this very interesting since I also saw books on stands in the astral, although my experience was different in that I couldn't consciously read them on the astral. In his case he could, and did so frequently as he was a history buff, and found that looking through these akashic records was quite enlightening. Kriyananda often said that history as we are given it is seldom anywhere near the truth; it is usually only a very dim reflection of truth, or a total fabrication.

In the astral, a book is an artificial form, and for many of us, the primary symbol of knowledge, even though we have many other physical ways to access knowledge. Probably now more people are seeing astral computer screens performing the same function, the symbols of knowledge interface changing as our culture changes. Personally I prefer the jewel-encrusted books to astral computer screens, but whatever works!

Over time I discovered many ways that worked for me, using different symbols and working at different levels, to access the akashic records. They can be accessed simply through direct intuition, or with the mediation of entities such as geniis, devas, spirits, gods and goddesses, as well as symbolic books and computer screens. It all depends on what sort of interface is comfortable and appealing to us.

Books Can Make You Famous

Despite the ceaseless warnings about the spiritual dangers of the ego and being full of oneself, I still like to indulge in mental scenarios where I am someone other than who I am, or at least I tell myself that I am pretending to be someone who is other than I am. In fact this someone is indeed a part of me, though not mostly who I am (I hope). I call this my inner bink.

In the context of higher self and a lower self, my inner bink resides firmly within my lower self. It surfaces most often when I am bored or doing tasks that I generally do not like.

My inner bink loves fame, fortune, and the pleasures of the world. It says stupid things and makes me feel smart when I do.

To a certain extent I actually enjoy my inner bink. We are all actors to some degree, and my inner bink allows me to play roles that are not very politically correct. And, after all, consider that if it wasn't for Shakespeare's inner bink, we probably would not have all those sharp-witted plays.

It was one of those mornings where I could barely wake up, and I realized I needed the incentive of some novel entertainment to get myself going. I peered into the bathroom mirror, and it suddenly occurred to me that I wanted to be famous. I said out loud, "Yes! I need fame."

As I readied myself for another day of work, I amused myself with thoughts of fame and how to get it. From the bathroom I proceeded to the couch to perform sockasana. For those not acquainted with esoteric terminology, an asana is a seat or position that you assume while doing hatha yoga or meditation. And, sock is a sock, something to put on one's foot. The high point of sockasana is when you have got one sock on, and you pause, hanging there with the other sock in hand before the final movement of applying it to the other foot. It's a mystical balance point of pure now, neither the beginning nor the ending.

As I looked up, steadying myself for the final move, I noticed a very thick occult textbook at the bottom of the bookshelf near the couch I was sitting on.

The book called to me. I lost my momentum in the mystical balance point and was distracted from completion of sockasana.

I stood up and picked up the very weighty tome. I'd had this book for a year or so and never really looked through it, always putting it aside, waiting for the availability of a large chunk of time proportional to the mass of the book.

Hefting it to the couch, I randomly opened the book and glimpsed what looked like my name. I gulped. It was my name, and they spoke of me in glowing tones.

There I was with only one sock on, barely awake, only about five minutes from requesting fame and here it is on the first page I open to. What more can you ask for and receive before your morning shave?

Astrology

Ions and the Bicycle Rider

It was sunny and pleasantly warm, and I felt great, having just left the classroom upon completion of final exams. I sat at the bus stop and opened a book up to read for pleasure, savoring the fact that I was not studying for a class. My mind soon became deeply immersed in the text, my eyes directed ground-ward into my book. Then, in the periphery of my vision there appeared a pair of bicycle wheels. I did not look up as I did not want to be disturbed, and I continued to read intently, ignoring the bicycle and cyclist.

But, the cyclist would not be ignored. "Do you go to school here?"

Without looking up I replied, "Yes."

He then said, "You know the last world war was caused by ions?"

I really didn't want to be bothered, but I figured I had better look up and find out who this nutcase was. At that time, the mid-1960s, one seldom saw an adult riding a bicycle, and discussion of ions was pretty much confined to science classes. I barely knew what ions were. O.K...

I reluctantly lifted my gaze to see a pleasant-looking fellow of about 40 standing in front of me, smiling. Not knowing what else to do, I smiled and waited for more enlightening historical tips. I didn't want to upset him as I presumed he was a bit of a loon even though he seemed harmless enough; and my bus was not due for a while yet, so I had no convenient means of immediate escape.

As I expected, he launched into a non-stop exposition about his theory of ionic concentration and polarity in the air, and how this affects people's thoughts and activities and causes world events. After around ten minutes it occurred to me that what he was saying could actually have some basis in reality.

About five minutes later he suddenly wrapped it up and said, "You should research this when you have the time. I think you will find it worth your while. Have a good day!" He grinned and pedaled off.

"Well, that was interesting," I thought to myself. "Ions?"

Several months later, in one of his lectures, my guru Kriyananda stated that the best time to meditate was on a clear, sunny, dry day, because under those conditions there are abundant negative ions in the air. I immediately remembered the bicycle rider at the bus stop.

At that moment I realized that I had to go to the library and read everything I could get my hands on about ions.

This led me to the work of A.L. Tchijevsky, a biophysicist, and founder of the science of heliobiology and aeroionization. His work included the study of the effect of ions on moods and health, and the fluctuation of ions due to solar flares caused by planetary configurations, among other things. As I stitched these various pieces of information together I realized that the guy on the bike was really onto something.

My further reading revealed that fluctuations in the geo-magnetic field due to solar flares and ionization had a lot to do with weather, states of human consciousness, and events on many levels. Ions, solar flares, planetary configurations... for me, it all pointed to astrology.

It was my good fortune that my guru's branch of the Kriya lineage included a lot of astrologers. Kriyananda was an as-trologer, as was his guru Shellji. Sri Yukteswar, guru of Para-mahansa Yogananda, was an astrologer of renowned in India, who crafted magical astrological amulets. As an initiate, these rich resources of the Kriya lineage were at my disposal, and my compelling desire to learn pushed me to dive deep and become totally immersed in this wonderful magical science.

I learned about the movement of the Sun, Moon, and planets through the signs of the zodiac, and how these celes-tial events affect the flow of energy in and out and through the chakras. Kriyananda taught me how to capture this ce-lestial energy and put it into talismans, just as Sri Yukteswar had done, to harmonize how we experience these cosmic cycles, and to help to further our spiritual awareness.

My primary subject for astrological study was myself, of course. After all, I was with myself twenty four hours a day, so my own experiences provided the most opportunities to study the cycles of astrological aspects and their correlation to the turn of daily affairs.

My study soon led me to became a professional astrologer. My first client was a Catholic priest, oddly enough. He had a genuine interest in esoteric sciences, and was quite enthusi-astic about having his chart read, despite his religion's stated position that astrology is the work of the devil. He seemed to really get a lot out of the reading, and I was thrilled that my first client was so satisfied.

I gained experience quickly over a short period of time, casting and reading many people's charts. (Bear in mind that all the calculations were done by hand. This was before the advent of computers with astrological software.) I was able to help my clients understand and make some order for themselves in what they were experiencing as a chaotic world. And, I got a lot of positive feedback, which further motivated my astrological pursuits. Sometimes, however, the feedback took odd forms.

Thank You But No Thank You

One of my clients suggested to a friend that she should have her chart read by me. The friend made an appointment and I calculated her chart. She was very congenial and pleasant, and we hit it off very well, I thought. But, about ten minutes into the reading she suddenly opened her handbag, pulled out her checkbook, scribbled furtively, and literally threw a check at me as she got up and rushed for the door. She had not said a word and I was totally dumbfounded. I managed to get over my initial surprise before she got to the door, and, worried, I asked if there was something wrong.

She looked back, still moving toward the door, and said, "Oh no! Everything is fine. You are a very good astrologer and as a matter of fact, too good. Everything you said about the details of my past was spot on. It's just that I don't think I can handle hearing about my future. I'm sorry, goodbye, and thank you," and she was gone from sight, never to be seen by me again.

I'm sure that I learned as much from reading charts as my clients did from my readings. I would spend about a week off and on meditating and studying each chart before I saw a client, which made me psychically sensitive to their patterns of vibration. At the reading, with the feedback loop between the client and me, I could make adjustments on the fly as I listened to and felt the client and got a better understanding of the exact circumstances of their life. I could correlate what was being presented to me at many levels by the client with the particular astrological configurations laid out in their chart. Thus, for me, each reading became a live presentation illustrating astrological aspects – combinations of planets and signs literally personified. I soaked up all this knowledge like a sponge.

Reading for clients was a rewarding practice, for the most part, but, it had its down sides. Astrology is not an indicator of fate any more than a weather report is. It is a tool that, when given its due, shows us how to overcome obstacles and navigate competently through all the layers of maya that human life consists of. Astrology will not, however, change a stupid person into a wise one, anymore than it can change a frog into a prince.

An astrologer can advise, but the client has to have enough understanding and the will to put the advice into practice. In order to change the trajectory of the karma coming at us, we must be able to transcend the self to some degree by whatever means is available. Some people naturally have this capability and some do not; and some with this understanding and capability decide, for whatever reason, not to use it and just let the karma run even though they could easily step off the tracks where the freight train is barreling toward them.

Red Sails in the Sunset

The most blatant example of this was a client I had who was a recreational sailor. Bill had a good-sized boat and loved to take it out on Lake Michigan as often as he could.

He had a prominent Sun opposed Uranus with a lot of other inharmonious, accident-prone aspects in his natal chart. This indicated to me that he would be likely to take his boat out in challenging weather conditions.

People with natal Sun opposed Uranus have a tendency to move ahead forcefully and willfully, according to their own wishes with no regard for reason, and little circumspection. In dangerous situations, this recklessness is likely to put them in harm's way, resulting in major injury or death.

One of the first things I said to Bill at the chart reading was, "Do not, absolutely do not, take your sailboat out in thunderstorms!"

I should not have been surprised with his response, but I was.

He said, "Oh, but I LOVE to take my boat out in thunderstorms!"

I shook my head, and said, "Well, it may be a great adrenaline rush and all, but you have a Sun opposed Uranus in your natal chart, which indicates to me that you are prone to get struck by lightening, which could make you very dead.

"At least let me give you some dates when the transiting planets indicate heightened danger for you, and then you can stay off the water if the weather seems at all electrical on those dates."

I gave him a list of specific dates.

Several months after the reading a friend called. About fifteen minutes into the conversation she said, "Oh, did you hear about Bill – he just died!"

"What happened? He was only in his early twenties."

She said that he deliberately took his boat out on the lake during a major electrical storm and got struck by lightening.

I almost dropped the phone at that point. "When did this happen?"

Sure enough, it was on one of the days in the list I had given him.

As I said earlier, astrology cannot change a stupid person into a wise sage.

Astrology can show us how to avoid outcomes we do not wish for, but it does not do the avoiding for us. We have to do that. And, in order to be able to apply the knowledge this science has to offer, it's necessary to be able to take a somewhat detached perspective of oneself, to step back. A regular meditation practice is helpful to achieve that sort of detachment, and indeed astrology (called jyotish, literally "light" in Sanskrit) is a powerful siddhi, the fruit of dedicated meditation and study.

Astrology reveals the past, the present, and the possibilities of the future – *trikala* ("the three times") in Sanskrit. A person skilled in discerning past, present and future is what Tantrics call a *trikala jnani*, "knower of the three times."

The siddhi of knowing astrology informs us that everything in this universe is actually quite orderly and not chaotic. Everything moves on a trajectory through time and space and has a relationship to all other flows of energy, objects and events. These relationships can be expressed as geometry, the ever-changing angular relationships of celestial bodies expressing one level of our orderly universe.

If we understand this science, we can shape and change events in our lives, soften difficult karma, and transform our selves.

Being an astrologer has its aggravating and humorous, (in hindsight) moments.

Alexander The Great

One person came to me and had decided that I should be his personal astrologer; however, he did not want to pay for my services. He implied that he was about to become such a fabulously great personage that I should be more than happy to do this work for him without recompense. I was not impressed, and needless to say I passed on this "great opportunity."

Blame it on Astrology

Michael had been studying astrology with me. He was a musician and part of a folk music trio.

One day I happened to be walking along the street with Sam, one of the other members of said trio. I was acquainted with Sam but did not really know him well.

I sensed that he was disturbed about something, and I asked him what was wrong.

"Well, Michael keeps showing up really late or not at all for practice, and he says it's because his astrological aspects are not right. Why did you have to go and teach him this crap? We can't get anything done as a band these days!"

I immediately knew what was going on. Michael was an epic procrastinator, astrology or no astrology. I had never known him to be on time for anything. He was referred to by those who knew him as a person who would be late or a no-show for his own funeral, and had a hard time keeping any job because of his consistent tardiness or absence.

If I found myself in a position where I needed to do something with him I always factored in two to three hours later than agreed times; and also that the planned event might very well not happen, at least not with Michael present.

I was not pleased to hear that Michael was trying to blame astrology for his extreme problem with schedules, and it was not too cute either that Michael had diverted Sam's considerable anger and frustration in my direction. It was quite palpable as we were walking along.

I refused to let myself or astrology in general to be scapegoated for Michael's major character defect.

"Astrology did not make Michael irresponsible; he made himself irresponsible. He's just using astrology as an excuse for his very own bad behavior.

"If he really was using astrology, he would avoid making appointments at bad times as much as possible in the first place, so there would be no need to cancel or be late."

Anyway, I rambled on in defense of astrology as we walked along, and after about a half hour it felt like I had mostly convinced Sam that I and astrological timing had nothing to do with his problems with Michael.

The Good News And The Bad News

It's always a high point when you can be the bearer of good news. The natal chart and transits of one of my clients looked to me like he could make a fortune by becoming an author.

"But, I've never written anything professionally!"

"Doesn't matter. Just find a subject you like, and write a book. It will be very, very successful, you'll make a lot of money with it."

During the rest of the reading I felt that he was taking my advice seriously, but was a bit perplexed as it had never occurred to him to pursue a career as a writer.

About a year and a half later, he came for another reading, and informed me that he had published his first book, a tourist guide to Chicago. It was so popular he had already made a million dollars just from the first printing.

Then sometimes there's bad news. One client was wondering whether her very hot, charming, on-again, off-again, Latin lover would return after dumping her. What I could see in her chart indicated that he was not coming back, and I had the unpleasant task of informing her of this.

I knew from her chart that she was an incurable romantic, and most likely could not admit to herself that he was not the type to roost in one nest for very long, and he was gone for good. I later got the distinct feeling that she did not get anything out of the reading and just wanted to remain wrapped up in her romantic fantasies and fixated on this guy.

Initially I felt sad for her about it; but there are thousands of people out there you can fall in love with and have a relationship with, so why waste your energy on unrequited love? But, then I realized she was very much enjoying her romantic fantasy… and why not, what's the harm? It's probably a step up from reading romance novels to pass the time.

Another client constantly phoned me to ask advice about the most inane things. It got to the point where every time I walked by the telephone I would almost break out in a rash in fear the phone would ring with yet another stupid question. But, out of this aggravation came a pearl. I actually sat down and invented my own system to answer questions on the fly fairly accurately without much work at all.

The system was ingenious, if I say so myself, and thus armed I now waited eagerly for her next intrusion.

She was right on schedule with her daily dozen questions, but this time I was able to immediately answer each question on her list. I could feel that she was flummoxed by the speed of my responses.

Before she could even complete asking a question, I gave her the answer for it and was ready for the next question.

She phoned one more time about a week later to tell me that my predictions were quite accurate. She fired off a few more questions, which I again responded to rapidly… and after that I never heard from her again!

In a way I was disappointed since I was now prepared to deal with her queries, come what may, any time of the day or night, with great ease.

At any rate, I had been forced to invent an accurate and easy-to-implement technique because of her annoying habits, so I now had at my fingertips a tool I could use with anyone, or for myself, to answer questions at a moment's notice.

Exploring Other Dimensions

As you progress in raising kundalini, you become aware and consciously active in other dimensions of time and space. There's more information about the rough divisions I use (etheric, astral, mental, and causal) of these other dimensions in the appendix of this book.

Projecting your consciousness into these other realms – call it astral projection, out-of-body-experience, remote viewing, whatever – is definitely a siddhi, and one that has resulted in some pretty amazing experiences for me.

Seeing My Own Body

The first time I saw my own physical body, looking pale and lying inert during an etheric projection, I was frightened and wondered if I was dead. The shock of it sent me right back into the physical. But, after the first few times I became quite at ease with it.

At times the extremities of my subtle body (feet, legs, hands, arms) feel as if they are floating upward, and I can move them while remaining motionless physically. I also sometimes feel my subtle body turning around in my physical body, even to the point of being upside down.

Once, as I was coming out of a projection, I felt as though my body was paralyzed and I could not even open my eyes. At first I panicked, but then I realized that it was just that it would take a little while to readjust to physical plane consciousness. But then, I felt someone's hand under my head, and I could not open my eyes to see whose it was.

Now I really panicked because I thought that in the physical, somebody had entered my house and, seeing me on the bed, they put their hand underneath my head to see if I was alive. The thought of a stranger doing this while I was unable to move at all was unnerving.

I reasoned that my only hope was to try to bring life back to my limbs without the intruder noticing. I decided to start wiggling my toes and work upward. However, once I was able to wiggle my toes, to keep them from returning to seeming paralysis, I had to wiggle them more and more vigorously, which was sure to reveal to the intruder that I was awake. I feared they might do harm to me, but I had no choice and decided to take my chances. After a minute or two I could open my eyes. When I did, I saw nothing. No one was in the room.

What I thought was a hand was really pressure at the back of my head that I was feeling in my etheric body. Needless to say, I was very relieved to not find the imagined physical intruder, although I felt rather silly about this little drama and laughed to myself, thinking how very easy it is for us to scare ourselves, though understandably so.

Etheric Vignettes

On another occasion, I lay down for a routine meditation. My head hit the pillow, my eyes closed, and immediately my etheric eyesight kicked in. I thought for a second that my eyes had suddenly opened or that I had forgotten to close them. I could see everything in the room just as it would appear to my physical eyes, except for one thing. To the right of my bed a tall figure in a cowled black robe was standing, looking at me, with its face obscured by the dark hood. I was rather terrified by this sinister-looking apparition right next to my bed. I opened my eyes and the figure had vanished. I stared at the spot for quite a while, wondering, "What the heck?"

The etheric is so close to the physical plane vibration that it can cause confusion and embarrassing moments. Many times I would get up out of bed in the middle of the night to relieve myself, only to realize that I was in the bathroom in my etheric body only, trying to do the impossible. On one of these occasions I solemnly walked back to my bedroom with a rather sheepish grin. I lay back down in my body, opened my eyes and got up to do it the right way.

Another time, right after falling asleep, I found myself suddenly awake in my etheric body. I was standing in the dining room staring at a very bright, glowing white light similar to that of a carbon arc lamp, only more subdued, on top of my dining room table. I could look straight at it without disturbing my vision, but I felt the presence of someone or something standing next to it.

I couldn't see who was standing there because of the intensity of the ball of light, or because they were not visible at the same wavelength that my consciousness was at the moment. I became afraid, although there was nothing particularly ominous about the apparition. It seemed to me that someone had just walked into my dining room, ball of light and all, and started mucking around. I stood at the entrance to the dining room and decided that I should order the entity and their sideshow out of my quarters.

I attempted to lift my arm authoritatively and point at the ball of light and its owner. But, lifting my arm took a huge effort. I strained, and managed the gesture, but my movements were much slower than I wanted them to be, and I realized I was not achieving the authoritative demeanor I had intended. I was annoyed at this difficulty of movement, but I also had an urgent feeling that I did not want whatever this thing was to know that I was a klutz in my etheric body.

Then, etheric arm raised, and finger pointed at the ball of light, I tried to say, "Be gone from my house," but I could barely move my tongue and lips and no sound was forthcoming. I struggled ferociously to get the words out of my mouth. Finally, sound emitted from my etheric mouth – very strained and low-pitched. It was so hard for me to speak that I felt like I was in a movie run in extremely slow motion. This was embarrassing because it completely blew my authoritative stance.

Just as I thought to myself that I had completely lost it and must appear foolish to whomever was there, I immediately found myself back in my body. In my physical body, I got up and ran to the dining room, expecting to still see this phenomenon; and, ready and able to give the interloper a good physical trouncing. When I reached the dining room, however, there was nothing out of the ordinary to be seen. I stood in the doorway for a few minutes looking around before retiring for the night in an uneasy state.

At first I was disturbed that I did not have control over my own household environment. However, the next day I felt more relaxed about the incident, and a sense of wonder came over me. What was it? I have never seen it repeated again, so I guess I will never know.

Remote Viewing

One night while sleeping, I awoke in my etheric body. I found myself in a dimly-lit part of the etheric, standing over a bin. Inside the bin were many hats, the type that uniformed people wear, with shiny leather bills on the front. The odd thing was that all the bills were cut off the caps. As I stared into the bin, I could not help but think that this was really stupid. I tried to figure out why the bills would be cut off and was very perplexed and amused. I came back to my body, opened my eyes, laughed, shook my head and went to sleep.

During the next few weeks I thought often about the bin with the silly-looking caps. This projection was particularly interesting to me because I intuitively knew that it was a etheric plane projection at a certain wavelength where everything would more or less be seen as it is with the physical eyes, but I could not understand how or why the bills would be cut off the caps. This part of the etheric is a region that relates closely to physical plane actualities, and where symbolism is uncharacteristic.

Although you do see many things on the etheric that you do not see on the physical, somehow I knew that the caps were not symbolic, but actual physical things. Still, I could not work out why someone would cut the bills off the caps and throw them in a bin.

I forgot about the incident until several months later when I got a part-time job with a clothing manufacturer. On my first day, I walked through the tailors room to the uniform department in the back. As I was looking around, I put my hands on a bin on the floor, about three feet high. I leaned over to see what was in it and was shocked. There, in the bin were the very same caps I saw in my projection, with the bills cut off. I found out that the caps were being reprocessed and it was common to put new bills on old hats.

In a sense this was a minor incident, but it really was a major step in gaining the ability to discriminate in the etheric, and it was powerful because of the very specific physical plane confirmation that I got later. In analyzing this experience, one could say that two siddhis occurred at the same time: precognition, which told me where I was going to be and what I would see in a matter of months (sort of time travel, if you will); and etheric projection (out-of-body experience), proof that our consciousness is not locked into the body.

Social Life in the Etheric

On another occasion, I woke up from a deep slumber to find myself having sexual intercourse in my etheric body with a woman I did not know. The projection was very conscious and intense. It only lasted for about ten or fifteen seconds. Whoever this woman was, I knew that she was a living person and had projected in her etheric body or was dreaming. Whether or not she was conscious of what she was doing, I do not know. She certainly seemed very conscious. While trying to not make a fool out of myself, I discreetly tried to see who it was that I was so closely and pleasantly engaged with. The light was dim. I craned my neck slightly to look at her face, but I immediately shot back to my physical body.

I opened my eyes with a smile on my face, and wondered who my midnight visitor was. I got up, had a cup of coffee and pondered. I had a suspicion that she was someone I knew, but I was not able to confirm it. Investigating such things can be a little awkward!

From several of my other projection experiences I knew that, at times, other people would be involved in my projections, yet in waking, they would not remember the dream or having projected. At other times people would see me and talk to me in projections, and they would remember and I wouldn't. There were times when we would both remember; and even sometimes when two or three people would meet me on the astral in projections or dreams, and we would all remember the experience.

We all seem to participate in events on the astral and etheric that we are not consciously aware of. Some of these events may be learning experiences. Others may be just friendly get-togethers; or sometimes we get together to work out problems with people.

I often have awakened in a projection, talking with physical plane friends who are also dreaming or in a conscious projection. One night I found myself dancing around a tree stump with two other friends, as if we were children having a very good time. The next day I asked each of them if they remembered their dreams, and they both had some recollection of our mutual etheric activities.

Past Lives and Spiritual Teachers

In one projection, I came upon a dying soldier clothed in luminescent chain mail. I watched him for a while and suspected that the soldier was me in a past life. The scene evoked no emotion in me, and I'm not really sure it was me dying, but it was a vivid and very interesting experience.

Another time I projected into a room that I felt to be my bedroom, though it was completely unlike where I lived in the physical. The bed was built into a wall, with ornately carved woodwork all around it. I had never seen anything like it before.

Months later, I came across a picture of exactly the same type of bed and woodwork, which was from a particular Chinese era. I have a feeling that my astral experience was a scene from a past incarnation, but am not sure.

At one point, I decided to search on the astral for a legendary spiritual teacher who supposedly will appear to those who call out for him. I was speeding through a beautiful ocean of light and called out his name, but as soon as I did this, the light dimmed and I slowed down, sinking down towards the etheric and into increasing darkness. Instinctively I put pressure on my third eye, and as I did, I rose upward into brighter regions; then, I called his name again, and once again descended into darkness. After several rounds of this with the same results, I gave up trying to find this astral guru and returned to my physical body. I did like the new third eye technique I had just learned for navigating; but I never did find that particular spiritual teacher on the astral.

Getting Around in the Other Worlds

On the whole, the astral and etheric planes are inter-esting and pleasant places, but there are regions that one should instinctively know to stay away from. I have had projections to what I can only describe as dark regions, which have the unpleasant quality of slum-like city scenes. They are dirty and filthy, populated by seamy characters with bad vibrations.

When I come upon these types of astral neighborhoods, I immediately "up" my vibrational frequency by putting pres-sure on my third eye, and the scene dissolves. My surrounds go out of focus, and I then find myself in brighter, more pleasant regions.

These dark regions are specific parts of the lower astral and etheric where people work out rough karma, just as they do in the physical world. The inhabitants are souls and enti-ties who are not quite up to snuff.

I have popped into some unusual scenarios when project-ing. One afternoon I found myself gazing at a human skel-eton laid out upon a stone slab. I observed for a while, from a distance, then suddenly, the skeleton began to move. I was quite startled by the movement and immediately found my-self back in my physical body. What this astral scene was all about I do not know. I had no sense of who it was or why I was seeing it.

One intriguing experience that I chose not to pursue oc-curred during my usual afternoon meditation practice. The energy surrounding me had been charged for several days, as I had been working with and meeting a lot of new acquain-tances involved in occult matters. I was quite excited and my mind was running on many different tracks at once.

I lay down, and in a matter of minutes I felt that I was being pulled upward into dark surroundings, as is usual during my etheric projections. It was like going through a tunnel formed by a whirling vortex. Suddenly, I was standing in deep water over my head, looking upward to the surface of a well. The well was made of and surrounded by stone, and in some sort of garden. There were six or seven figures that seemed like monks, standing in a circle, leaning over and gazing down upon me in the water. They were dressed in robes and chanting intently. I could not make out what exactly they were chanting, but their efforts were definitely focused on me.

It felt strange to me to have this group making me the center of their attention. I had no idea whether the situation was good or bad, but I was not comfortable with it. They saw my face in the pool and became excited, smiling to each other as if they were proud that their evocation had worked so well.

The apprehension of not knowing what was going on threw me back into my body. I kept my eyes closed, regained my composure and mulled over the strange group.

I was still in a state where I could project again, so I did. Again through the darkness, the vortex, the well. I could see their faces coming closer and closer until I was right there again, and they were still chanting and watching me through the surface of the water. I immediately came back to my body. Although I could have projected again, I decided against it, as I had no idea what these people were up to and for some reason did not want to push it. I got up and went about my daily tasks, pondering the incident and wondering whether or not they would show up again sometime.

Often, on the astral, scenes dissolve around me, and give way to different environs. The change of scene is sometimes accompanied by a flying or rocketing sensation. At times I have felt that I was flying at very great speed, and at other times I simply flow gently from one region to another.

Many of my projections include this sense of flying. One night as I left my body, I was frightened by the great speed with which I was being pushed outward. But, fortunately my curiosity was stronger than my fear, so instead of holding myself back, I faked a brave stance and yelled "Superman!" in my mind as I was ejected outward in a dark whirlwind upon the cosmos.

Oddly enough there are times when I am so tired that I just want to sleep a very deep sleep, and not be bothered by projection experiences. One night as I lay down, all I could think about was the quiet peaceful sleep I had been looking forward to at the end of a very long day.

My head hit the pillow, and I found myself going out of my body – a very easy and very fluid exit. I found it ironic that this should be so when I really only wanted to sleep; and, when I was really interested in projection, it required so much more effort on my part. I got up and decided to have some tea, then went back to bed, but the same thing happened. The minute my head hit the pillow, I started to slide right out again. I got up and repeated this cycle – tea, lie down, project, get up – about six times before I could fall asleep without projecting. It was quite ironic considering that, at the time, I was putting as much effort and time into projecting as I possibly could; but, this particular night I was so tired that I would have none of it. I would have gladly traded all my astral kingdoms for a good night's sleep. There have been many times since when I have recalled this incident and wished I could duplicate the ease and swiftness of release I experienced when I didn't want it!

The Astral Kitchen

One of my more humorous projection experiences occurred one afternoon after I lay down for my routine meditation. It took about a half hour for me to be on my way; but then I shot out of my body at great speed. There was a gradual slowing down, and a scene began to crystallize around me. I found myself in a kitchen – a very pretty kitchen, absolutely picture perfect, with sparkling appliances and a curtained window by the sink. I like to cook and appreciated the charm of the scene. As I looked around I began to wonder whether I was in a physical plane kitchen or an astral one. After a while it seemed to me that it must be the latter. Everything was radiant and very crisp. The colors were too vibrant and too perfect to be physical. Also, there was not a single object out of place, and one rarely sees that on the physical, although I have heard rumors of immaculate kitchens.

On the table in the center of the kitchen there was a bowl. I peered into it and saw several eggs which I presumed were about to be cracked and mixed.

The sense of being an intruder crept over me and I worried a bit about getting caught here; but, the scene seemed so pleasant that I told myself that whoever lived here would be glad to receive me.

Suddenly, a stocky middle-aged woman came in through the kitchen door. She had a startled and very angry look on her face and demanded to know what I was doing in her kitchen. Before I could reply, she lunged towards me, screaming at me to get out of her house.

I attempted to tell her who I was, but her yelling was nonstop and evidently she had no interest in what I was trying to say. She reared back and slapped my right cheek. The well-placed blow sent me right back to my body.

I opened my eyes and still felt the slap's effect, physically. It was a rather unusual feeling, not one of pain, but a physical sensation that lingered for about fifteen or thirty seconds. So much for astral hospitality. I surmised from this incident that, at times, intrusions are no more welcome in the astral than they are in the physical plane.

Astral Flashes

During meditation, as kundalini rises, I sometimes get what I call astral flashes. These are quick flashes of scenes, faces or light that are three dimensional and very brightly colored. While still in the body, you are, for a fleeting moment, seeing into the astral.

Faces of different kinds seem to predominate at times. Some are grotesque, others beautiful or humorous. Swami Sivananda calls them Shiva's attendants and has noted that they are there to test your strength and courage, but they are totally harmless. Swami Lakshmanjoo also mentions them in his works.

One may also see beautiful scenes with bright colors. Sometimes these are accompanied by sound: loud crashes, bells, voices, rushing whirlwinds, buzzing and clicks. The sounds can be real foolers because they are etheric sounds that you can hear quite distinctly, and you would swear they are physical sounds, though they are not. All these phenomena are normal and you get used to them.

One night in meditation I was attempting to create knocking sounds on a nearby desk. Suddenly there was an awful din of furniture banging against the floor, so loud that it seemed like there was a huge earthquake and the house was being shaken to pieces.

But, there was someone else in the room, also meditating, and they did not hear a thing.

I had managed to create a large commotion with my experiment, but only on the etheric and not the physical plane, even though it sounded physcial to me.

Still, you can create real physical sounds during meditation. At times I have gotten physical knocks and raps, and sundry other phenomena that were apparent to others and not just myself.

A wide range of physical sensations can occur when I meditate and attempt to project, such as an isolated part of my body getting hot or cold, or feeling as though it's moving slightly when the rest of my body is still. This is related to astral and etheric currents, and loosening the etheric body from the physical. It's all harmless, and it is fascinating to try to figure out what each experience is about.

Oceans of Light

On some astral journeys, or in an astral flash, I have encountered a brilliant white light. Sometimes this light is accompanied by a buzzing or crackling sound almost electrical in nature, and at other times there is no sound. What this light is I do not know. When I have confronted it I have chosen not to walk into it. It felt and looked quite awe-inspiring. I have never felt any menace or negativity about it. I have simply felt that it was not my time to go there. I have met other people who have told me the same thing, but I have never met anyone who says they have walked through it.

As my projection experiences continued, I found myself projecting into oceans of light, flying through them effortlessly.

On one occasion I was flying through a sea of beautiful green light. Suddenly, on the horizon coming toward me was a vast expanse of large white globes, as far as my astral eyes could see. It felt to me like some type of barrier or demarcation. I did not go through it, and came back to my body.

I decided to ask Kriyananda, who knew about such things, what the significance was of the globes and sea of beautiful green light. He said that I had been in what is called the Venusian sphere, and the white dots or globes are what the ancient Quabbalists called Paroketh, "the veil," a demarcation between the Venus sphere and the upper regions on the Tree of Life.

He gazed into the air with a vacant look on his face and said, "Hmmmm. I'm surprised you got that far."

Not knowing whether this was a put-down or compliment, I decided to let that conversation go and moved on to other questions I had for him.

Causal Experiences

Some projections occur beyond the etheric and astral planes. These are regions of higher vibration known as the mental and causal planes.

During one afternoon meditation I was thrown into what appeared to be a vast and deep space. My intuition told me that this was the causal plane. Then, I began to descend into what I can only describe as a seemingly infinite web-like network of lines of force. I felt that this was the mental plane just below the causal. By intuition I realized that the converging lines of force were actually me and my connections to what surrounds me on all planes of existence; and, that in fact we are what surrounds us. As I descended further down and back into my physical plane bedroom, I actually understood and felt that, in a sense, my environment and I were one and the same. This was an extremely profound experience.

As I opened my eyes, I could still feel these connections and I contemplated them, in awe of what I had just experienced and learned. The simplest way I can put it, is that what we normally think of as "me" and "not me" are, from a certain plane of perception, one and the same. It occurred to me that we are literally walking within ourselves, so to speak.

Another causal plane projection occurred one night when I was first learning the *Vajra Vidyut* technique. I had been lying down for perhaps two minutes or so, when suddenly, I was in a totally different space than I was ever in before. It was a complete void, and I do mean void. Being in deepest space would not be as much of a void as this was. I could see nothing because there were no objects to see or feel. It is hard to convey, but it was not that I could not see because there was no light. Indeed, there was no light, but

I could still see (or feel) that there was nothing whatsoever to reflect light if there had been light. I thought to myself that there are billions upon billions of miles of nothingness somewhere in this universe and I was experiencing it. This was truly a deep void with nothing but me in it.

I became extremely frightened, because as an ego creature, there was no-thing to relate to, not even a very distant star.

I immediately came back to my body in stark terror. I bolted out of bed, glad to see simple objects, anything I could relate to. I was perspiring profusely and my heart was racing. This was my first glimpse at nothingness. It took me numerous cups of coffee and several hours to steady my nerves. It was a bit much for a mere mortal to comprehend.

There was nothing really threatening or bad about the experience, but humans are accustomed to having things to relate to mentally, emotionally and physically. Our sense of self is supported by things that seem to be not-self reflecting back at us. When the whole rug is suddenly pulled from beneath your feet (and there's no floor either!), the experience is extremely profound, and terrifying.

The next afternoon I projected again. This time I literally found myself being a star, much like our own sun. A very grand ego, to say the least, and around me were other stars that I could relate to. The experience of knowing that I and every other soul in this cosmos is actually a star is a feeling that is hard to explain, but one thing I can say, is that it balanced out the void of the day before and felt very good. I came back to my body with a big smile on my face.

Shopping for an Incarnation

It should have come as no surprise to me because I live in a consumer oriented society, but I must admit I was a bit taken aback to discover that we can actually shop, choose and order up a life scenario for our next incarnation.

I was enthralled with the presentation given to me on the astral. It consisted of a large number of viewing screens or blocks of scenarios, as if you had 30 or 40 TV sets or computer screens in front of you, each playing a different channel. As my attention went to a screen, it would animate and I would be drawn into the surroundings and ambiance, a "virtual reality" immersion on steroids – but this was infinitely more rich in things to experience.

I instinctively knew that I could choose any one of these scenarios for the theme of an incarnation if I so desired.

When immersed in one of these previews of a possible incarnation, it was a total surround experience with the taste, touch, smell, feel, sounds and sights of the environment and the major theme and characters in play. Each preview had a powerful attraction and I could see how easy it would be to be pulled into various incarnations time and again because of the allure of these situations.

This projection itself was a truly profound experience for me, but what really capped it was a statement my guru made during a lecture several months later.

"Some people will actually incarnate just for a beer."

Everybody in the audience laughed, but he looked at the crowd and said, "You laugh, but I'm serious. There ARE people who incarnate simply to have a beer."

Anybody for Munich during October Fest? Reincarnation can cure what ales you!!!

Everything is All Right

It only lasted for about a second, but the effect is still with me. I was sitting at my desk in front of my computer and thinking my usual various mundane thoughts when suddenly an intense awareness broke through my thought-stream. All brain chatter, angst and physical tension fell away, leaving only a profound feeling and knowing that everything was all right.

Everything was fine and going the way it should. I became extremely calm and felt really, really good. Samadhi, for real!

A Thought in Closing

Siddhis come to us for very good reasons. They are gifts, and part of our spiritual evolutionary process. But, in some ways, gaining siddhis is like opening Pandora's box, so it is wise to remember these words from the *Katha Upanishad* :

Rise, awake!
Having obtained these boons, understand them!
Like the razor's sharp edge is difficult to traverse,
the path to one's Self is difficult.

— Katha Upanishad, 1.3.14 ,
Translated by WD Whitney

In meditating upon that statement, it has occurred to me that the most important siddhi is the intuition which guides us through our daily life to the best positive outcomes for us and others around us.

Appendix

What are Siddhis?

The Sanskrit word *siddhi* means perfection, accomplishment, attainment in any endeavor. In the context of yoga practice it usually refers to the attainment of a magical power beyond normal human experience.

Siddhis are presented in the writer Patanjali's synopsis of yoga practice, popularly known as Patanjali's *Yoga Sutras*. There are many other ancient Indian texts that mention other siddhis, but the eight listed by Patanjali, the *astasiddhis*, are the most well-known:

1. *Anima* - The power of becoming small

2. *Laghima* - The power of becoming light

3. *Mahima* - The power of becoming big

4. *Garima* - The power to become heavy

5. *Istva* - The power to control universal processes and events

6. *Vastva* - The power to subjugate all

7. *Prakamya* - Irresistible will or fiat

8. *Vyapti* - The power to pervade the whole universe

When I first read this list of siddhis years ago, I burst out laughing.

"Right, make myself big – what, like *Godzilla* or *The Attack of the Fifty Foot Woman*? Or, make myself small, like *The Incredible Shrinking Man*?" (I like B grade movies...)

It all reminded me of a circus sideshow, and of when I was very young and saw one whopping huge giant at the circus. He made a lasting impression (fortunately only mentally) when he raised his foot outward and up to show the audience, and barely missed kicking me in the head. He had a very huge foot that you would not want to be kicked with.

So much for a reverential reading of ancient texts.

I settled down into a slightly more studious mood, and considered that I really do have a western mind and am thousand of years and thousands of miles removed from the context of the *Yoga Sutras*.

At first glance some of the astasiddhis seemed rather stupid. Who would spend years of their lives in intense discipline to make themselves big or small?

Well, at times walking through some neighborhoods in Chicago I admit I have wished for either that get-small or get-big power.

There are people (fakirs, for example) who spend many years working for one such siddhi or another. And, in the south of India there are traditions of the *siddhars* or *siddhas*, people who are considered miracle workers of sorts, among other things.

As I read and digested available manuscripts, I found that the archaic manner in which siddhis were presented did little for my modern comprehension and understanding of the reality and nature of these powers and capabilities.

My own spiritual discipline had brought me smack-dab into the world of siddhis under the guidance of my guru Goswami Kriyananda, who indeed could be called a siddha. I had some experience of the real thing, and I was becoming aware of a considerable disconnect between the ancient literature about the nature of siddhis and how to achieve them (and the current understanding of that literature); and my own experience and observations as part of a living lineage. Lost in translation? Or, perhaps some of the ancient scribes didn't have much of an understanding of their subject in the first place…

Perhaps a contemporary voice could make all this more relevant, understandable and achievable for the average person. There are modern stories of siddhis in action, amazing and true, here with us today and maybe right next door to where you live.

Still, it seems to me that it is somewhat easier for people to accept the reality of "supernatural" abilities if the context is the distant past or far-away exotic places. Distance in time and space makes such events less threatening to the consensus view of day-to-day reality; but siddhis conveyed as they really happen in a contemporary environment, in my experience, seem to be more difficult for people to integrate into their world views.

Beyond Patanjali's list, siddhis include phenomena such as materialization, psychokinesis, levitation, precognition and projection of the consciousness (often called etheric or astral projection), clairvoyance, clairaudience, as well as time travel into past and future probability events, and much more. These categories are not discrete – a mix of phenomena, such as precognition and projection of consciousness is more typical, in my experience.

The Other Worlds

For the yogi, there are other dimensions of time and space to be experienced, beyond our physical plane, waking state of consciousness. As you pursue your practice of meditation and your kundalini rises, the door to this other world opens up for you.

Today even science approaches these realms, as quantum physics and superstring theory point to a universe of many more dimensions than the present scientific model accounts for. These other dimensions of time and space are at least as vast as our physical universe. Sri Yukteswar, one of the gurus in our lineage, stated that they were hundreds of times larger than our total physical universe.

Historically, the "other worlds," (the dimensions beyond the physical) have been thought of as the places of heavens and hells, and the abodes of gods, devas and angels. Every culture has its own way of speaking of and relating to encounters with this other-world region; and these experiences spawn religious or spiritual structures of myth and ritual to explain, describe and relate to the phenomena. Religious texts are essentially the documents of the attempts of a culture to explain and categorize encounters with the "other world."

In the West, the other world is referred to popularly with catch-all terms such as the astral plane or the "other side." Buddhists refer to it as the *bardo*, or the regions of *stod* and *bar*. In ancient Egypt some called it the *tuat*. Hindu traditions divide these other dimensions into a series of levels called *lokas*.

As an example of a more detailed break-down, some Hindu sects divide the other world into fourteen lokas (dimensions) with each of us having as many koshas (sheaths or bodies), that is, a specific part of human consciousness and human function, that inhabits each loka. Within Hinduism there are many variations on these divisions, depending which tradition you are communicating with.

In Egypt divisions of the tuat were defined by their relation to the portion of the tuat that they called *sekhet aaru* or *sekhet hetepet* as defined in *The Book of Gates* and *The Shat Am Tuat*. In earlier versions the divisions were seven in number, but later versions included further divisions into twelve and twenty-one. The Egyptians posited that we were composed of many different sheaths (like the koshas of Hindu sects) that inhabited the tuat: *ka, ba, khaibit, ku, khat* and so on; but, no one is entirely clear about the mechanics or designations of these sheaths/bodies.

Each system of any of these different cultures has its own attendant god forms (gods/goddesses), creatures, guardians and so forth, which correspond to the culture's particular divisions and sub-divisions of these other dimensions of time and space.

The key is to understand that all of these formats, and the forms that populate them, are real and valid. They are built-up thought forms created from extremely pliable astral material arranged via physical plane ritual by practitioners of various traditions. This phenomenon has caused much confusion for esoteric students down through the ages, as the students inevitably try to figure out who's in charge from their own particular religious point of view. In fact, nobody's in charge but yourself. Any esoteric system is valid to the end that it serves, but beyond that, you're on your own.

The objective energies of the lower regions of the nonphysical dimensions can be molded to act according to the subjective transcendental ends, intentions, and perceptions of a culture, group or individual. However, this is true only in the denser, lower vibratory areas of the non-physical dimensions. The deep roots of our consciousness are in the higher, more universal archetypal forces in the upper regions of these invisible worlds.

As these more abstract, universal energies pass through the denser regions of the non-physical dimensions, they become more individuated and take form according to the perceptual constructs of groups and individuals. So, if you are a Buddhist, and upon your demise you feel that you need to be punished for various errant acts that you have committed, then you will get exactly that when you hit the astral. If you happen to be a Christian and believe that you should be rewarded for your behavior in this life, then you will get the works – choirs of angels, harps and wings... the whole nine yards.

Essentially, whatever system you buy into with your beliefs will tend to, at least for a while, throw you into a region of the astral that supports your vision of the cosmos. The what and the why of this process has filled many volumes of esoteric philosophy.

I like to work with a simple four-fold division of the "other" dimensions of time and space. This model is one used by many swamis, gurus and modern occult teachers and researchers. It is not perfect, but it is a useful framework for practical understanding. It's a simple rough guide, and, if you explore these regions, as you grow with experience you will likely redefine a framework according to your discoveries and make your own divisions. You will also understand and experience why certain traditional divisions are there already.

If you wish to use a more detailed framework and have the time, there is an enormous body of literature available for study on the subject from a variety of spiritual traditions.

The Five Divisions

We are essentially pure consciousness, and we have locked ourselves into certain vibratory rates to complete tasks for a purpose we have yet to discover, ofttimes called karma. According to our model we perceive and act through five different bodies, or vehicles, on five different planes of existence.

The divisions of these planes of existence that I use are: causal plane, mental plane, astral plane, etheric plane and physical plane.

The physical plane which we inhabit has the slowest and densest vibration. It is the physical plane that our consciousness is locked into most of the time.

Of the non-physical planes, the causal has the highest vibratory rate and the etheric, the lowest, just above the range of our physical sense perceptions. We inhabit all of these planes simultaneously in our various bodies, but in our normal state of consciousness we are usually only aware of the physical plane through our physical body's sense perceptions.

On the causal plane, we perceive and act through our causal body. On the mental plane, we do so with our mental body. The same occurs with the astral, etheric and physical. Each body is limited to a specific range of vibration that it can perceive.

As pure consciousness, we act and perceive in different dimensions of time and space. Each dimension of time and space has its own logic or logos. Each logos operates through a range of frequencies which we will call vibratory rates.

Many esotericists speak of raising or lowering the vibratory rate. This is quite correct and describes the process of consciousness entering and leaving various dimensions of time and space. Although, for simplicity's sake, I use such terms as "above," "below," and "high" and "low;" these are highly marginal descriptors and do not really describe any kind of spatial relationship. For instance, I use "above" for planes of higher vibratory rate, and "below" for those of lower vibratory rate, relative to other dimensions of time and space, but in fact, each one of these dimensions coexist, one within the other.

Along these lines, I also use the word "projection" to describe the transference of consciousness to other regions or dimensions in time and space. In general, my use of words that imply a physical spatial relationship is simply to help create a model that our physical plane consciousness can grasp. If you find this confusing, don't worry about it. It is of no consequence unless you want it to be.

Remember that words are no more than signposts and guides – they don't fully and accurately represent the phenomenon. There are many ways to describe, evaluate and compartmentalize experience; but what really matters is to experience these dimensions of time and space.

Etheric Plane

The most dense plane beyond the physical is the etheric, and it is the substrate for the physical plane. The appearance of this region is often shadowy with very little light. Projections into the etheric often have a dull, gray quality. An etheric projection can result in many types of experiences, depending upon what portion of the etheric we are talking about.

The most common type of etheric projection or experience is simply leaving the body and flying or walking in the physical plane. Any type of out-of-body experience in which we see and operate on the fringes of the physical plane can be called an etheric projection.

As we ascend to higher regions of the etheric, physical plane scenes fade away and we enter a truly different time and space location. We find both the familiar and the strange: populated cities and towns with people working regular jobs; or alien landscapes and scenarios populated with a variety of odd creatures – and everything in between.

In the higher ranges of the etheric, moving toward the astral, the scenes become brighter and more light-filled.

Astral Plane, Upper and Lower

The lower astral, like the etheric, is populated with a variety of phenomena. In the lower astral our subconscious meets archetypal energies descending from the upper astral. It is to the lower astral that we go when we dream, for the most part. Dreams are semi-conscious astral and etheric projections. Since the astral is composed of an extremely fluid substance, we can create all manner of situations for ourselves, and this is usually reflected in our dream states.

We are very active on the astral while our physical body sleeps. We visit with friends, work out problems, converse with other entities and learn many things. It is in the astral that we refresh ourselves and make ready for our next day on the physical plane. This is one reason why sleep is so very essential for us. On the astral we can make adjustments to physical and etheric circumstances, and we can change the nature of events to some degree.

The upper astral is quite beautiful, with vast oceans of light. These oceans of light each have a certain vibratory rate and related states of consciousness associated with them. The Quabbalists call these the Sephiroth in the Tree of Life. To travel through these vast spheres of light is quite an experience in a fully conscious projection. Each sphere is a different color, and the color is a signature of the quality of consciousness related to it.

Mental Plane

Above the astral is the mental plane where ideas that develop and materialize in the astral, etheric and physical are first manifest. All ideas are generated on the mental plane. The lower mental is connected with our mind and mental processes, just as the lower astral is connected with our states of feeling and emotions.

The archetypes, origins and templates of all manifest things are in the mental sphere.

Causal Plane

At a higher vibratory rate is the causal plane. Here, cause as we know it has its origins. On the causal, time and space are one. Object and observer come together and the oneness of the uni-verse is comprehended. There are also multiple levels of the causal plane, but they have to be experienced to be comprehended.

All of the experiences I discuss in this book relating to different dimensions of time and space were not drug in-duced and occurred while I was totally conscious. They were the direct result of practicing *Vajra Vidyut* technique as a spiritual discipline.

A Reading List

In no particular order, here are some books to read on your way to cosmic consciousness, from my book genii to yours.

Swami Sivananda - *Spiritual Experiences*, Shivanandanagar, Uttarakhand, India: The Divine Life Trust Society, 1957

Swami Sivananda - *Kundalini Yoga*, Shivanandanagar, Uttarakhand, India: The Divine Life Trust Society, 1935

Shri Dhyanyogi Madhusudandas - *Shakti: An Introduction to Kundalini Maha Yoga*, Antioch CA, USA: Dhyanyoga Centers, 1979

Shri Dhyanyogi Madhusudandas - *Light On Meditaion*, Scotts Valley, California, USA: Keshavdas Karl Kuntz, 1976

Goswami Kriyananda - *Extraordinary Spiritual Potential*, Chicago, Illinois, USA: The Temple Of Kriya Yoga, 1988

Paramahansa Yogananda - *Autobiography of a Yogi*, Nevada City, California, USA: Crystal Clarity Publishers, 1946

John Blofeld - *Mantras: Sacred Words of Power*, New York, New York, USA: E.P. Dutton & Co., Inc. 1977

Yram - *Practical Astral Projection*, London, Great Britain: Rider & Company, 1926

Henry Steel Olcott - *Isis In America*, New York, New York, USA: Penguin Group, 2014

Alexandra David-Neel - *Magic and Mystery In Tibet*, New York, New York, USA: Dover Publications, 1971

Louis Pauwels and Jacques Bergier - *Morning of the Magicians*, New York, New York USA: Stein And Day 1964

Dean Radin - *Supernormal: Science, Yoga, and the Evidence For Extraordinary Psychic Abilities*, New York, New York, USA: Deepak Chopra Books, 2013

Dion Fortune - *Psychic Self Defence*, London, Great Britain: The Aquarian Press, 1967

Russell Targ - *The Reality Of ESP: A Physicist's Proof of Psychic Reality*, Wheaton, Illinois, USA: Theosophical Publishing House, 2012

Dale E. Graff - *Tracks In The Psychic Wilderness*, Boston, MA, USA: Element Books Inc., 1988

Sylvan Muldoon and Hereward Carrington - *The Phenomena of Astral Projection*, London, Great Britain: Rider & Company, 1951

Franz Bardon - *Initiation Into Hermetics*, Wuppeertal, Western Germany: Dieter Ruggeberg, 1976

*"**Herbal Alchemy** integrates magical practices with laboratory work."*

The Complete Golden Dawn System of Magic by Israel Regardie

Herbal Alchemy
by Phillip Hurley

When originally published in 1977, *Herbal Alchemy* broke new ground as the first straight-forward written pre-sentation of Alchemy in a complete, practical form - as science, art, technique, philosophy, magic and spiritual practice. In this revised and updated edition, Phillip Hurley provides detailed information about the preparation of alchemical elixirs from plants, the application of astrology to herbalism, and reveals secrets of occult ritual practice in the Tantric, Hermetic, and Quabbalistic alchemical traditions.

www.herbal-alchemy.com

Tantra, Yoga of Ecstasy:
the Sadhaka's Guide to Kundalini and the Left-Hand Path

by Leigh Hurley & Phillip Hurley

Tantra is an ancient discipline with deep cosmic roots Every movement in time and space is ritual for the Tantric sadhaka, and every moment is a moment of transmutation, of alchemy. Shiva and Shakti bring us back to first principles in a feeling way that engages all of our senses, and all levels of our being. The Tantric sadhaka is enlightened by the manifestation of these first principles in their life - physically, psychologically, sociologically, and spiritually.

Tantra, Yoga of Ecstasy details ritual, practice, meditation and psychology for the serious student of Tantra.

Topics discussed include:

- ॐ Meaning and intent of classical Tantric rituals
- ॐ Tantric philosophy
- ॐ How to raise kundalini
- ॐ Shiva-Shakti meditation and Tantric initiation
- ॐ Tantra, art and creativity
- ॐ Alchemy of personal transmutation
- ॐ Deciphering the puzzle of Tantric morality
- ॐ Tantric use of astrology

www.tantrayoga.us

Namarupa:
the Magic of Tantra Mantra

by Phillip Hurley & Leigh Hurley

Namarupa is an initiation into mantra yoga, complete with detailed Sanskrit pronunciation, alphabet and calligraphy guides. All mantras are presented in Devanagari script with English transliteration for easy reference. Written from the perspective of the tantric sadhaka (practitioner), Namarupa presents the esoteric meanings and uses of the mantras and alphabet; and discusses mantra sadhana both as classically practiced and updated for modern life. Of special interest are detailed Tantric mantra techniques for raising kundalini, previously available only to initiates.

Namarupa: the Magic of Tantra Mantra includes:

- ॐ Sanskrit letter portraits
- ॐ Sanskrit quick reference tables & pronunciation guide
- ॐ How to initiate a mantra
- ॐ Japa, pranayama, and modes of chanting
- ॐ Detailed discussion of bija mantras
- ॐ Timing & rectification of mantras
- ॐ Deity, planetary, directional & general mantras
- ॐ Mantra cycles for working with the five elements and raising kundalini
- ॐ Likhita japa and calligraphy guides

www.tantrayoga.us

Kundalini:
Tantra Yoga in Practice

by Phillip Hurley & Leigh Hurley

KUNDALINI
Tantra Yoga in Practice

Phillip Hurley & Leigh Hurley

This is an approachable, lucid and engaging guide to the philosophy of Tantra, and its techniques for raising kundalini. The authors have many years experience in spiritual practice and study as initiates under the direct guidance of Goswami Kriyananda, in the lineage of Shellji and his guru, Paramahansa Yogananda.

Kundalini: Tantra Yoga in Practice is a workbook with a wide range of clearly detailed and illustrated techniques for developing an effective personal kundalini practice. It is suitable for beginners, and as a class guide for Hatha Yoga teachers who wish to introduce and integrate kundalini meditation into their offerings.

Presented here are down-to-earth methods based on classical Tantric tradition and agamas. Includes:

- ॐ What is Kundalini?
- ॐ Raising Kundalini
- ॐ The Subtle Anatomy of Kundalini
- ॐ Svantantrya
- ॐ Karma and Maya
- ॐ Prepatory Practices
- ॐ Lifestyle Suggestions

- ॐ Yoga Nidra
- ॐ Tribindu Pranayama
- ॐ Working with Chakras
- ॐ Vajra Vidyut
- ॐ Upavestana
- ॐ Yajna
- ॐ Siddhis, Astrology and Kundalini

www.tantrayoga.us